ABORIGINAL LANGUAGES AND EDUCATION: THE CANADIAN EXPERIENCE

edited by

Sonia Morris
University of Saskatchewan

Keith McLeod
University of Toronto

Marcel Danesi
University of Toronto

MOSAIC PRESS
Oakville - New York - London

CANADIAN CATALOGUING IN PUBLICATION DATA

Aboriginal languages and education : the Canadian experience

ISBN   0-88962-479-8

1. Indians of North America - Canada - Languages.
2. Indians of North America - Canada - Education.
3. Native language and education - Canada.
I. Morris, Sonia V.   II. McLeod, Keith A., 1935-   .
III. Danesi, Marcel, 1946-   .

E96.2.A26 1993   371.97'97071   C93-094076-8

No part of this book may be reproduced or transmitted in any form, by any means, electronic or mechanical, including photocopying and recording information storage and retrieval systems, without permission in writing from the publisher, except by a reviewer who may quote brief passages in a review.

Published by MOSAIC PRESS, P.O. Box 1032, Oakville, Ontario, L6J 5E9, Canada. Offices and warehouse at 1252 Speers Road, Units #1&2, Oakville, Ontario, L6L 5N9, Canada.

Mosaic Press acknowledges the assistance of the Canada Council and the Ontario Arts Council in support of its publishing programme.

Copyright © 1993, the Authors
Design by Patty Gallinger
Typeset by Jackie Ernst

Printed and bound in Canada.

ISBN 0-88962-479-8 PB

MOSAIC PRESS:
In Canada:
    MOSAIC PRESS, 1252 Speers Road, Units 1&2, Oakville, Ontario L6L 5N9, Canada. P.O. Box 1032, Oakville, Ontario L6J 5E9.

In the U.K.:
    John Calder (Publishers) Ltd., 9-15 Neal Street, London, WCZH 9TU, England.

Acknowledgements

I would like to thank Professors Marcel Danesi and Sonia Morris for their participation in this publication venture. This project has taken longer than we planned; however, the response to the call for papers was more than anticipated. We divided the original concept into two so that we ended up with one book on Aboriginal Languages and another on Heritage Languages.

The three of us would like to thank the contributors who submitted the contents of the volumes. We would also like to thank Donato Santeramo and Frances Koltowski who assisted with checking the galleys. Lastly, we would like to thank Mosaic Press who have published the volumes.

Keith A. McLeod

Contents

Introduction	i

Essays

Robert M. Leavitt *Language and Cultural Content in Native Education.*	1
Augie Fleras *Preschooling with a Difference: A Maori Language Education Program in New Zealand.*	17
J.B. Frideres and W. J. Reeves *Indian Education: An Alternative Program*	37
Catharine Littlejohn and Shirley Fredeen *Indian Language Programs in Saskatchewan: A Survey*	57
Arlene Stairs *Learning Processes and Teaching Roles in Native Education: Cultural Base and Cultural Brokerage*	85
Mary Heit and Heather Blair *Language Needs and Characteristics of Saskatchewan Indian and Metis Students: Implications for Educators*	103
Richard Fiordo and Claudio Violato *Teaching Instructional Communication to Indigenous People in Alberta*	129

Introduction

The speaking and writing of aboriginal languages, and the maintenance of the cultures they circumscribe, are vital to the preservation of Canada's identity. In the expression of a deeply-reflective Weltanschauung, and in the codification of a rich tradition, these languages constitute precious verbal media for conveying and institutionalizing ideas, concepts, and emotions that relate to the experience of Canada in its ecological totality.

The key to preserving these languages is education--the teaching of aboriginal languages and their cultures in school, and their utilization as vehicles for the acquisition of knowledge and skills, especially in the context of the elementary school system where language plays a crucial role in the child's cognitive and affective development. This volume brings together seven studies, written by experts in the field, that deal with the most important features of native Canadian language education: the relation of language to culture; the kinds of curricular approaches best suited to aboriginal languages; the optimal pattern of relationship between teacher and learner; the linguistic characteristics of the learner; and the role of communication in language study.

The study by Robert M. Leavitt--"Language and Cultural Content in Native Education"--describes crucial differences between European and native language systems and between the European and aboriginal approaches to education. Essentially, the European approach to teaching focuses on specific goals and on the obstacles to be overcome to attain them. The aboriginal approach, on the other hand, is highly experiential with the eyes and ears focused on the educational process itself. Leavitt suggests that it is the teacher's task to help learners discover how to learn in the way that is most appropriate to the information to be acquired.

In "Preschooling with a Cultural Difference: A Maori Language Education Program in New Zealand," Augie Fleras addresses the issue of aboriginal language education by examining Maori efforts at renewal through the establishment of culturally-sensitive and community-based Maori language immersion preschools. The success and popularity of te Kohanga Reo reflects a commitment of community organization, a reliance on cultural values, and a willingness to collaborate. As such, Fleras' essay constitutes a valuable case study from New Zealand with obvious implications for the Canadian situation.

Friederas and Reeves discuss the nature of schools, their effect or impact upon Native students. In response to their observation that Native controlled schools do little better, they outline a program to improve both schools and post-secondary education.

The survey of Indian language programs in Saskatchewan (Kindergarten to Grade 12) by Catharine Littlejohn and Shirley Fredeen constitutes a knowledge base from which to extract Canada-wide models of curriculum and instruction. The two authors identify a need for the public discussion of the issues surrounding aboriginal language education in Canada: its role in school programs; its relation to other programs; the steps involved in implementing a program; etc. Clearly, the time has now come to develop a comprehensive system to support and encourage the educational use of Canada's aboriginal languages. The authors conclude their survey with a series of valuable recommendations as targets for discussion.

Arlene Stairs, in "Learning Processes and Teaching Roles in Native Education: Cultural Base and Cultural Brokerage" describes a study she conducted involving over 100 aboriginal university students, who were divided into: (1) subjects who lectured to a group of their peers for a designated amount of time (monological instruction); and (2) subjects who conducted a dialogue with a group of their peers within a specific time frame (dialogical instruction). The implications of her findings are discussed in the light of appropriate models of speech instruction to aboriginal students.

Mary Heit and Heather Blair--"Language Needs and Characteristics of Saskatchewan Indian and Metis Students: Implications for Educators"--examine the language characteristics of Indian and Metis students and the nature of the school programs that are presently available to them. They conclude by emphasizing the need to allow such students to develop facility with language in as wide a variety of functions, styles, and registers as possible, since this is the primary means for empowering these students.

Finally, Richard Fiordo and Claudio Violato look, in "Teaching Instructional Communication to Indigenous People in Alberta" at the benefits of one-way versus two-way models of oral instruction in aboriginal education. Their study has found that the two-way model for teaching speech communication is a highly workable one.

The educational issues discussed, together with the pedagogical principles and practices described in this volume, are of obvious value and relevance to the education of aboriginal people in Canada and to the maintenance of their languages and cultures. Hopefully, this volume will be of practical use to educators, teacher trainers classroom teachers, and researchers in the field as a point of reference. To the best of our knowledge, no similar volume exists, and we sincerely hope that it can help to expand the educational discourse on aboriginal language learning and teaching in Canada

LANGUAGE AND CULTURAL CONTEXT IN NATIVE EDUCATION

Robert M. Leavitt
University of New Brunswick

In the summers of 1987 and 1988, a course on the cultural implications of teaching English and native languages to native Indian and Inuit children was offered at Concordia University in Montreal. Experienced teachers and teachers-in-training (both referred to hereinafter as "teachers") enroled in the course, each group including both natives and nonnatives. Only one of the nonnative teachers had previous experience in teaching native children. A few others intended to work in native education, but most were planning careers in teaching English as a second language to other linguistic groups. Originally, the course was intended simply to help teachers explore methods of teaching native languages and English, and to offer nonnative teachers insights into the problems encountered by native children in learning English as a second language. It became apparent during the first summer, however, that the course was accomplishing more than this. Both native and nonnative teachers were beginning to see the significance of language and culture in children's schooling. Working closely with their classmates of the "other culture", they found themselves reevaluating and reshaping their own roles as educators. This and the article by Arlene Stairs will explore the outcomes of that experience.

The instructors conducted the class as a model of traditional native educational practices at work (see Briggs 1983, Cronin 1982, Erickson

& Mohatt 1982, Macias 1987, Modiano 1975). They were able to demonstrate the effectiveness of an approach based upon active participation, student-initiated exploration of selected materials, and planned student-instructor collaboration. In addition, they arranged for participants to hear of firsthand experiences with native education from a number of Inuit, Ojibway, and Mohawk guest speakers, as well as from Indian classmates. Lectures were kept to a minimum, in favour of small-group and whole-class discussions, presentations, and workshops; course grades were based equally upon individual and group achievement. To make the purpose of their approach clear, the instructors frequently took advantage of opportunities to step back from the experiences in class and to analyze what the teachers themselves were doing.

The written evaluations at the end of the course confirmed that something of importance had taken place. Participants emphasized the value of their involvement in discussions of cultural identity and relationships. "The input for me came mainly from my native classmates, both professionally and personally", commented one teacher. Another wrote that the course opened up "social, political, and cultural discussion of what maternal languages mean, in ways the regular TESL courses do not."

Their discussions, the presentations they heard, and their research and writing helped teachers discover how traditional native education relies upon ways of knowing, ways of interacting, and ways of using language which are not normally exploited in formal schooling (for example, conceiving of time as sequence rather than duration, collaboration between children and adults, storytelling and oral history). They saw not only that these "ways" are the basis of culturally appropriate education for native children, but also that they offer unique alternatives for meeting the needs of nonnative children. How the language and the content of traditional native education might find a place in the classroom is the subject of this articles.

Native teachers began to articulate the dilemma they face in "trying to regain both knowledge and understanding of our language and culture" within the context of a European model of education. As they explored ways in which native language and content might be used in the classroom they at first thought it feasible only to alternate native and nonnative approaches during the school day; not until later did they consider ways of melding the two. One native-language teacher commented upon the necessity of trying "to sort out differences in value systems and religious beliefs that have been tying us to different worlds without completely letting us into either one." How, for instance, might myths and legends be used as lesson content, respecting their sacredness and honouring their fundamental truth, while at the same time helping children analyze then from a critical point of view to discover native knowledge and values? One native teacher related how she had been told a set of stories as a gift from an elder so that she might share them with her students; the students in turn became aware not only of the content of the stories themselves but also of their place in the linguistic culture of their community.

Nonnative teachers, in working with their native colleagues, discovered the extent to which native languages, value systems and traditional educational practices contrast with their own. They realized that they would have to learn about the first language and culture of *any* children they taught--and would have to account for these in their teaching. One teacher wrote that she had become aware of her responsibility to "look at how a native child develops in her own culture. The child will carry with her the theory of teaching and learning embedded in the native culture. She is trained for autonomy and self-reliance and to have many and varied relationships with peers and adults". Another teacher warned that by trying to reshape native customs and beliefs to fit into a dominant-culture mould, "educators are changing the whole idea or definition of the term 'native' of 'original peoples of Canada'". He recognized the power of education to create new perceptions and a new culture, and the responsibility teachers assume for shaping students' identities.

Culture-Based Education in the Classroom Setting

The course approached the methodology of teaching native students as a search for the ideal balance between maintaining a native way of life and achieving economic and political independence. These goals, which have been set by Indian and Inuit peoples themselves (e.g. Charleston 1988: 71), are not mutually exclusive, as might at first appear. Teachers can address them jointly, however, only by taking into account the continuous development of native culture from the past to the present and by considering all aspects of the culture that exists today in Indian and Inuit communities:

> · *Material culture:*
> is ordinarily the sum total of "native content" found in school programs. It includes the objects and skills pertinent to a people's ecology and economy.

- *Social culture:*
  has implications for classroom interactions: How do teachers' roles fit into the patterns of personal interaction, communication, kinship organization, and other relationships with the community?
- *Cognitive culture:*
  has implications for the organization of program content: What are the characteristics of individual and collective world view, value systems, spiritual understanding, and practical knowledge?
- *Linguistic culture:*
  consists of the role of language in community situations. It includes how language is used (stories, gossip, conversation, negotiation, etc.) and how language maintains individual and group identity and transmits material, social, and cognitive culture from one generation to the next.

To account for all four aspects of culture, the instructors emphasized the necessity of basing education *in* native culture, rather than simply including components of material culture as content (see Stairs, the volume). Few teachers have had the opportunity to address more than the material level of native culture (or the culture of any English-second-language pupils). Even where curriculum pays heed to social, cognitive, and linguistic culture, it is almost always from a material point of view. Spiritual beliefs and legends, for instance, are treated as artifacts, and these, together with descriptions of kinship patterns, transportation and hunting techniques, and the names of languages, tools, and food plants, make up a static set of information about Indian and Inuit peoples. With few exceptions, the educational principles and practices of native cultures are not applied in the classroom setting, even for native students.

But classroom teachers can use the social, cognitive, and linguistic aspects of native culture. Rather than simply presenting material culture under the title of "native studies" or an "Indian unit," teachers in a culture-based program will look at their own interactions with children to see where and how they might modify their formal teaching. In particular, how might English and the native language be used in the classroom? What content will be appropriate in a culture-based curriculum and how might it be organized most effectively (see Stairs 1988)?

Language in Native Education

For teachers, the most significant differences between English and the Indian and Inuit languages are to be found in their ways of conceptualizing, preserving, and transmitting knowledge. Until very recently, the native languages have developed entirely in the oral mode. Speakers hold in their individual and collective memories everything that they know and believe about the world and their experiences in it. Always accessible, either in speakers' own minds or through direct conversation with others, knowledge and beliefs have an immediacy not readily apparent to speakers of written languages, who use writing and reading to store and transmit much of what they know (Gill 1982).

Literacy, which puts some distance between spoken words and the reader or writer, makes possible--indeed encourages--the extensive analysis and reworking, sorting and classifying of ideas, including those gleaned from the writings of others. Writing creates distinctions between facts and beliefs, between ideas and feelings--distinctions which are significant to scholars in general, as well as to those who work in fields such as jurisprudence, applied sciences, or documentary history. For example, the present essay, which attempts to derive generalized principles about native education by analyzing a set of events and other writings, together with the language emerging from the would not be "told" in an oral tradition. Rather, the discussion might take the form of multifaceted conversation and narration about the teaching of native children, presenting accounts of many experiences and resulting in a conceptualization of ever-increasing completeness, without a stated conclusion. Neither approach is superior to the other, but each has its advantages in given situations. Therefore, it is possible to embrace literacy as a creative, rather than destructive, adjunct to the oral tradition. Teachers can facilitate this helpful blend, however, only by acknowledging the value of both components.

In the actual case, the ascendancy of spoken English and English literacy in native communities in Canada has threatened not only the oral tradition, but also the survival of native languages themselves (Burnaby 1986, Foster 1984)--peoples' ways of thinking, communicating, and establishing an identity. In some cases, the intruder language has undermined oral tradition by imposing a new reliance on writing for the authentication of knowledge and ideas. In native communities, however, the transmission of a distinctive culture still depends upon the maintenance of native languages in their oral mode. Myths and legends, for example, are seldom, if ever, told in English, and the lessons they contain about history, human relationships, proper behaviour, and universal truths are thus lost to younger generations. To overcome this loss, one teacher in the Maine-Maritime region engaged her students in a bilingual study of the contrasts between their grandparents' childhoods in the 1920's and their own in the 1980's. She compiled transcriptions of stories told by elders into a book (Socobasin 1979) and told stories herself as a way of presenting the lessons to students. At the same time she showed the children how the contrasts they were discovering related to broader changes in the region--as found in written histories and diaries, census data, church records, and other archival documents, including maps and photographs. The teacher, her students, and the adults in the community gained a clearer understanding of the continuing role of the oral tradition in their lives.

Literacy in the native language holds the promise of providing a bridge between the oral tradition and English literacy. Until recently, however, written native language has been used mostly in the nonnative fields of journalism, formal education, and religion--in transcriptions of news and history, myths and legends, songs and liturgy--and only tentatively in the creation of a distinctive literature. There are, however, exceptional circumstances which suggest the potential of such a literature. As it develops. it encourages writers to take their language in new direction. Young Inuit, for instance, become literate in Inuktitut not only from classroom instruction, but also by reading and writing with their parents and grandparents, who use syllabics in personal correspondence. Inuit elders discussing education have added another use for writing to the native-language repertoire, saying that traditional knowledge and skills "should be recognized in paper". Several published life stories are now being used widely in Inuktitut education, demonstrating to students the vitality and cultural appropriateness of many types of literacy.

A series of Micmac writers' workshops held recently in New Brunswick and Nova Scotia resulted in three volumes of stories for readers of all ages (Metallic and Metallic 1985, Milliea 1985, Leavitt, Francis, and Paul 1986). The contents ranged from traditional tales and classical mythology to fantasy and personal reminiscences. Each submission was carefully scrutinized by native editors, who took pains to ensure that it met standards of good oral expression, but who at the same time wished to encourage innovations. They accepted poetry and a playscript, neither one a traditional form, but each true to Micmac culture in its style, wording, and point of view--and thus a "logical" modern extension of the oral tradition.

Defining the roles of oral and written language in children's education should help teachers determine the best use of the language in classroom interactions. In Micmac community schools in the

Maritime provinces, for example, Micmac teachers have been using the native language regularly and comfortably, but for the most part only on the periphery of education activities--in giving directions, maintaining order, chatting informally with children between classes, and occasionally in clarifying ideas the children find difficult in English. How else might it serve the goals of formal education? One teacher in Cape Breton has had her students tell stories in Micmac as a way of practising the language and learning appropriate forms of communication. Their stories become the basis of writing and reading activities in follow-up lessons, and of planned interviews with adults. Because the teacher herself also tells stories and writes and conducts interviews in the community, the children are naturally steeped in real-life language use. Speaking Micmac in a specific context has become for these children a productive way of learning to communicate.

The teacher who uses the native language in instruction becomes aware of how it differs from English. This kind of metalinguistic perspective helps her to understand the native language as a valuable complement--not a detriment--to the students' English. Her knowledge of the native language tells her, for example that while children may be able to use shapes and understand them in relation to particular objects, they may not be able to talk about them as abstractions.

In native languages, such basic notions as the shape of concrete objects may be expressed in ways unfamiliar to speakers of English, allowing a more effective view of the world for certain purposes. In English, for example, speakers consider the shape of a basket or a tree-limb (e.g. square or cylindrical) separately from the object itself; that is, the designation of shape is based on arbitrary or idealized forms, rather than on the properties of certain objects. Even with non-geometrical "shapes" such as *lump*, it is possible to picture *a lump* not made of any particular substance. In contrast, in languages like Maliseet, a close relative of Micmac spoken in New Brunswick and Maine, speakers perceive shape as a property of the object in question; it is expressed only as part of the noun or verb denoting or referring to the object. No shape-names are whole words, and Maliseet speakers do not ordinarily talk about shapes in isolation from the natural and manufactured objects around them. These different ways of thinking--Maliseet and English--are indicated not only in the lexicons, but also in the perceptions which form the basis of description. The single work *etutapskonuwat* ("he/she has very chubby cheeks") is a verb which describes someone's face by synthesizing the abstract concepts of "degree," "shape," "body part," and "state of being". In contrast, the English equivalent analyzes the face, expressing each idea--person, possession, degree, shape, body-part--in a separate word.

The Maliseet approach to shape is similar to that of the other North American native languages. At one level, it would appear, the child accustomed to a native system may have no use for simple geometric shapes. At another level, however, like Jennifer MacPherson's Inuk student Norman, who created a perfectly-scaled miniature dogsled, he may be capable of astounding feats of applied geometry. "Norman showed an extraordinary ability to deal with shape, with space, and with size, which seemed inconsistent with his general disinterest in the number-based mathematics we offered in school (MacPherson 1987: 25). Encouraged to develop the Inuktitut thought-patterns his work reveals, a student like Norman can approach everyday math problems with confidence. He can then use English to tell, for example, how he made his model, or how he will use it, and from there learn to analyze the model in abstract terms.

Shapes and other properties of material objects seem self-evident to speakers of any language, who do not question their inherent usefulness or their universality. In a similar way, relationships among events are understandable only in terms of one's own way of verifying the truth. For example, in teaching natural sciences, the English-speaking teacher will begin with the assumption that the moon and the wind are "things" which move, and whose appearance or strength changes with time. In contrast, Maliseet-speakers do not know the wind and the moon as things. There is no Maliseet noun "wind," but only a verb, which means "blow" or "be windy". The wind is not a thing, but an action. It can be named only be expressing this action--as when it is performed by a character in a story. Thus *Wocawson* is the name of the great bird who flaps his wings to make the wind. But he is not "The Wind": his names means "It Is Windy". When he blows too hard, the people can't go about their daily business, *Koluskap*, the culture hero, ties down one of his wings--weakening the action, but not the bird himself (*Koluskap naka Siwiyi*). The Indo-European perception is exemplified by Aesop, who presents the Wind as a person striving to make a traveller take off his cloak.

The moon is also named by a Maliseet verb--*nipawset* "walks at night". A multitude of other English nouns are expressed as verbs in Maliseet, including weather conditions, tides, land forms, and time. Thinking of these phenomena as actions helps students see their connections with other actions, including their own.

The ideas about shapes and natural phenomena mentioned here illustrate only a few of the fundamental differences in the thinking of people who speak different languages. They point to deeper differences in the nature of knowledge itself, in approaches in reasoning, and in the creation of new ideas. Speakers of North American native languages do not necessarily organize reasoning according to a linear sequence of causes-and effects, or axioms-theorems-corollaries, as do speakers of European languages. Instead they may keep a number of related ideas in mind, without assigning them an order of hierarchy. To linear thinkers, this approach may seem scattered and without focus. Native-language thinkers, on the other hand, may find logical sequences rigid and narrow, because they commonly approach an idea or a topic from many different directions. Norman's teacher would have approached model-making step by step, measuring distances and angles separately, then calculating the correct proportions to achieve an accurate representation of the original dogsled; Norman integrated all of these features without making any of them explicit to himself or to his teacher (MacPherson 1987).

Distance, angle, and proportion, treated as self-contained ideas, are abstract concepts derived from logical analysis of the physical world. In native languages, these attributes are specified only in respect to actual objects and relationships; the abstractions do not occur as words, as subjects for discussion, or as explicit considerations in perception. Similarly, there are no words meaning *size* or *colour*. Geography, mathematics, and fine arts are practiced--but not discussed as areas of study; the same is true of traditional native "disciplines" such as music, spirituality and history. Yet native people become well versed in these fields, and many even specialize in one of them. They come at the particular skills without having them isolated by teachers for practice and perfection. This approach to learning persists even among children whose first language is English, but whose parents' maternal language was Indian or Inuit.

In native communities, parents and elders maintain the integration of knowledge as they teach younger people by sharing experiences with them, by not isolating the knowledge and skills required by certain disciplines. Each skill has a social, economic, spiritual, and historical context. Children participate in the daily activities of adults, instead of practising in an artificial setting like a classroom. Knowledge about "fish-spawning", for example, is acquired not by taking biology or zoology, but through participating in what English-speakers might call travel, fishing, aquaculture, storytelling, economic development, history, art, environmental studies, law, and so on. From each repeated experience, the student learns more about fish-spawning, its relation to other natural processes and its "place" in society and in the ecosystem. There is, in effect, only one, all-encompassing subject and one, lifelong lesson.

Rather than organizing vocabulary or social studies curriculum by noun-centred topics, teachers need to look at each area of study in the context of the children's daily life. Inuit children, for example, do not spontaneously sort rocks by size, colour, shape, or mineral composition, they begin by considering which would be good for holding down tents, or for use as sinkers or projectiles. Children learn skills through experience with adults, not by having adults tell them what to do in recipe or instruction-manual fashion:

> You just had to watch your grandparents or your parents to learn (to knit Cowichan sweaters). No one taught me; I picked it up on my own. That was sort of a traditional way, for grandparents to let you learn on your own. They were just there to answer questions. You show it to them and ask if there's any faults. I guess that's where we spoil our children. We try to show them and now they're not interested (Irene Cooper, quoted in Meikle 1987: 13).

The implications for teaching are clear. Whether conducted in the native language or in English, whether they address manual dexterity, general knowledge, or skills like writing and mathematics, classroom activities will be most effective when centred on real life tasks, with children involved as apprentices. Children will also benefit from participation in meaningful projects outside the classroom. School becomes a place where in daily life they become better and better at all the skills required by their community--in the present and in the future. The teacher will think, for example, of the many contexts in which students can learn the history and geography of their community-- through hikes and canoe trips, map study, readings, oral history, road-building, religious and legal history, archaeology, mythology, hunting and fishing activities, agriculture.

Teachers of native students will want to inquire about the best situations for conversation, the most natural methods of description and classification, and real functions of language in their students' lives. They will want to let students integrate their experiences, spiritual beliefs, and social values with what they read and hear. Using this approach to language, teachers will be able to help native students find their way into the continuum of interconnections between the generations, between people and the world about them between the knowledge of individuals and that of the community as a whole. The dominance of verbs in native languages may be thought of as exemplifying the awareness of happening, eventuating, change, flow; literacy is making it possible to discover parts and distinctions, to distill and classify, to apply native language to nonnative ideas in areas such as science, law, government, and economic development.

ABORIGINAL LANGUAGES AND EDUCATION:
THE CANADIAN EXPERIENCE

THIS MATERIAL IS THE SOLE PROPERTY OF
THE CENTRE FOR LEARNING

RETURN TO:
Health Canada   HRDC
Suite 837 Canada Place   Suite 1440 Canada Place
9700 Jasper Avenue   9700 Jasper Avenue
EDMONTON, AB T5J 4C3   EDMONTON, AB T5J 4C1
Phone: 780-495-6567 or 780-495-4965 or 780-495-5884
ALL COSTS FOR ANY LOST, DAMAGED OR NON-RETURNED
MATERIALS SHALL BE THE RESPONSIBILITY OF THE
BORROWER.

English literacy is also making its impact on the social culture of native communities. Learning by reading (teaching with texts) is removing education from the realm of personal interaction and breaking the link between knowledge and the value system (Stairs, this volume). Teachers in the Concordia course became aware of their responsibility to maintain the kind of interpersonal communication--conversation, storytelling, talking-while-doing--which they find in their students' communities. Even where students work entirely in English, their personal relationships often retain features of the oral tradition, such as extensive, egalitarian peer interaction and collaboration. Like the Cowichan knitters, teachers cannot afford to be "showing" their students. They must let the students show them. Then English language and literacy, with its analytic point of view, will help both the individual and the community. Culture and identity change with the introduction of English, but the changes can be positive.

The Cultural Component of Programs

In comparing English-second-language and native-second-language curricula, the teachers observed that both have cultural content; that is, students are learning about the culture of people who speak English or a given native language. In the case of programs for native students, this usually means the inclusion of information in both languages about native material culture--artifacts, traditional skills, and related knowledge and beliefs--which is seen as essential to understanding the native way of like. Typically, this kind of content is presented as lessons in social studies, but perhaps also in art (native crafts and design), history (events and personalities), music (songs and dances), geography (territories and resources), language arts (legends and oral history), and other disciplines, such as religious or governmental studies. Including such content in areas of the school curriculum would seem to give validity to the culture native students bring with them into the classroom. The approach, however, segments native like in a nonnative way, by viewing it in English terms as a composite of specializations. This may happen even when the medium of instruction is a native language.

When instructing native children in English, teachers often strive to create a bicultural curriculum, one which takes into account both the mainstream culture and that of the community. The purposes of bicultural curriculum are to help students feel that the school program is a natural part of their lives and to help them move smoothly back and forth between one culture and the other. First attempts often focus on the attributes that native and nonnative cultures have in common, recognizing that native communities share many experiences with their neighbours. Much has been written and taught about the similarities and contrasts between Indian and non-Indian governments, clothing, religion, and decorative arts.

To make further progress towards appropriate native education, teachers must choose whether programs will simply include native culture as content, or whether they will be based in native culture through the adaptation of traditional educational practices. Only the latter approach takes advantage of what both cultures have to offer and helps students move confidently--using familiar processes--from what they know into the discovery of what is new and useful in English (Leavitt 1987).

The educational vocabulary of the Maliseet language is indicative of the greater native concern with process that with outcome (Carpenter, Varley, and Flaherty 1959). While modern English also treats education as a process (except for "pupil", the words in Figure 1 are verbs), it makes as clear dichotomy between the role of teacher and the role of learner. In Maliseet, however, there is only one very root, -*kehk*-, common to all the words listed. This root means "know", and it is combined with other roots and inflections to produce the works listed below:

English Word	Maliseet Word	Literal Translation
teach	ntokehkikem	I teach
teach something	ntokehkikemin (eli...)	I teach (how to...)
teach someone	ntokehkima	I teach her/him
teacher	nutokehkikemit	one who teaches
learn, study	ntokehkims	I teach myself
learn, study something	ntokehkimsin (eli...)	I teach myself (how to...)
learner, student, pupil	nutokehkimut *or* etolokehkimut	one who is taught *or* one who is being taught
my pupil	etolokehkimuk	one who I am teaching
school (education)	kehkitin	there is teaching
school (a building)	ihtolokehkitimok	where there is teaching
subject	ekehkitasik	what is taught
lesson	kehkitasu	it is being taught

In actual practice, a Maliseet subject or lesson has no existence apart from the teaching of it. Children do not learn "something"; they teach themselves how to do it by watching, listening, imitating, and participating. The Cowichan knitter quoted above saw herself not as having been taught, in the English sense, but as having "picked it up" (i.e. having taught herself). Her grandparents customarily let children teach themselves. For many native children, school instruction, with its assumption that children will "learn", has resulted in failure. In order to help their native students succeed, teachers must become models, not simply instructors.

An additional point of view on the differences between European and native pedagogies is expressed by a teacher from Kahnawake, Quebec, who contrasts the English maxim "If at first you don't succeed, try, try again" with the Mohawk version "Watch and listen and do it right, watch and listen and do it right" (Brisebois 1986). In the one culture, all attention is on the goal; the assumption is that it will be difficult to attain, but that the obstacles are worth overcoming. In the other culture, eyes and ears focus on what is happening now; this is the desirable strategy, successful in and of itself. These two maxims exemplify the contrast between education as the imparting of skills, knowledge, and content which will be useful in future activities--and education as the achievement of significant participation in ongoing adult work, where the content is the real-life task at hand.

Teaching must distinguish between what is creative and helps students inquire into and build upon their own experience and what is assimilative and consequently destructive. They must consider whether they are encouraging students to take English and use it appropriately within their own culture. Only as they develop an understanding of students' needs and knowledge of students' communities will teachers be able to find this ideal cultural balance in their work.

English offers new speakers a chance to see, as it were, new content in everyday experiences. Native students can learn that systems of distinct disciplines (law, spirituality, geography, history, economics) and the notion of "forces" or "elements" (historical continuity, the Crown, land use, economic clout) can be useful tools in managing experience, setting goals, becoming proactive, negotiating (for example, to define and defend land claims and hunting and fishing right). The teacher's task is to help students discover the information and "ways of knowing" accessible to them through English, as well as to recognize the insights their mother tongue has given them.

References

Briggs, J. (1983).
Le modèle traditionnel de l'education chez les Inuit. *Recherches Amérindiennes au Québec* 13:13-25.

Burnaby, B. (1986).
The Use of Aboriginal Languages in Canada: An Analysis of the 1981 census Data. Ottawa: department of the Secretary of State.

Carpenter, E., Varley, F., and Flaherty, R. (1959).
Eskimo. Toronto: University of Toronto Press.

Charleston, G., (ed.) (1988).
Tradition and Education: Towards a Vision of Our Future, Vol. 1 Summerstown: Assembly of First Nations.

Cronin, M. (1982).
Cree Children's Knowledge of Story Structure: Some Guidelines for the Classroom. *Canadian Journal of Native Education* 9: 4-12.

Erickson, F. and Mohatt, G. (1982).
Cultural Organization of Participation of Structures in Two Classrooms of Indian Students. In G. D. Spindler (ed.), *Doing the Ethnography of Schooling: Educational Anthropology in Action,* 132-174. New York: Holt, Rinehart & Winston.

Foster, M. K. (1984).
Canada's First Languages. *Language and Society* 9: 7-16.

Gill, S. D. (1982).
Beyond the Primitive: The Religions of Non-literate Peoples. Englewood Cliffs, N. J: Prentice-Hall.

Leavitt, R., Francis, B., and Paul, E. (eds.) (1986).
A 'tukwaqnn: Micmac stories. Fredericton: Micmac-Maliseet Institute.

Leavitt, R. (1987).
Fluency is Not Enough: Reassessing the Goals of Native Language Instruction. In W. Cowan (ed.), *Papers of the eighteenth Algonquian Conference,* 165-172. Ottawa: Carleton University.

Macias, J. (1987).
The Hidden Curriculum of Papago Teachers: American Indian Strategies for Mitigating Cultural Discontinuity in Early Schooling. In G. Spindler and L. Spindler (eds.), *Interpretive Ethnography of Education,* 34-51. Hillsdale: Erlbaum.

MacPherson, J. (1987).
Norman. *For the Learning of Mathematics* 7: 24-27.

Meikle, M. (1987).
Cowichan Indian Knitting (Museum Note 21). Vancouver: UBC Museum of Anthropology.

Metallic, E. and Metallic, A. (eds.) (1985).
Atugwagnn: Micmac Stories. Fredericton: Micmac-Maliseet Institute.

Milliea, M. (ed.), (1985).
Atogoagann: Micmac stories. Fredericton: Micmac-Maliseet Institute.

Modiano, N. (1975).
Using Native Instructional Patterns for Teacher Training: A Chiapas Experiment. In R. Troike & N. Modiano (eds.), *Proceedings of the First Inter-American Conference on Bilingual Education,* 349-355. Mexico City, 1974-1975.

Socobasin, M. E. (1979).
Maliyan: Mary Ann. Indian Township: Wabnaki Bilingual Education Program.

Stairs, A. (1988).
Beyond Cultural Inclusion: An Inuit Example of Indigenous Educational Development. In J. Cummins and T. Skutnabb-Kangas (eds.), *Minority education,* 34-53. Clevedon: Multilingual Matters.

PRESCHOOLING WITH A CULTURAL DIFFERENCE: A MAORI LANGUAGE EDUCATION PROGRAM IN NEW ZEALAND

Augie Fleras
University of Waterloo

Introduction

Aboriginal peoples throughout the world have taken the initiative recently in redefining their relationship with central authorities (Stea and Wisner 1984, Paine 1985, Little Bear, Boldt, and Long 1984, Dyck 1984, Frideres 1988). As indigenous occupants with special claims, the "nations within" have struggled to establish innovative political links from which to assert control over a broad range of concerns. Special attention has focused on the need to avert the further disintegration of an already threatened language base. Various strategies and programs have been proposed, but few have proven successful. Still, in view of the correlation between language, identity and achievement (Edwards 1985), the principle of aboriginal language renewal is resolutely endorsed as an indispensable right, not merely as an option or privilege (Shkilnyk 1986).

A similar situation prevails among the Maori in New Zealand. Maori aboriginal assertiveness has escalated with growing concern over the declining status of Maori culture and language (Awatere 1984, Greenland, 1984). A Maori cultural renaissance is now in evidence, propelled to a large extent by developments in language renewal at community and national levels. Of those innovations under this cultural renaissance, none have achieved the same level of publicity as the network of community-based and culturally-sensitive Maori language immersion preschools known as te Kohanga Reo (literally, 'language nests'). In contrast with conventional preschools and childcare centres, the Kohanga Reo employs te reo Maori (Maori language) exclusively as the medium of verbal interaction. Reliance on community involvement and an extended family setting (whanau) provides a learning context for the enculturation of Maori cultural values (Maoritanga). The impact of the Kohanga Reo cannot be taken lightly. It provides a tangible expression of New Zealand's incipient biculturalism and growing commitment to partnership perspectives between the founding nations (tangata whenua). Equally significant, the Kohanga Reo has drawn attention to the potential for alternatives in aboriginal language education both in New Zealand and elsewhere.

This paper will analyze the te Kohanga Reo from the perspective of a community-based and culturally-sensitive mechanism for language preservation within the broader context of Maori self-determination (mana Maori motuhake). Emphasis is focused on the influence of Maori cultural values--especially those pertaining to family and community--in sorting out the program's organization, content, and acceptance. The Kohanga Reo will be examined along several dimensions including: (a) historical background and social context; (b) cultural and community basis of its objectives, style, and operating philosophy; and (c) impact and implications for redefining Maori-government relations. This discussion is followed by a comparable if somewhat briefer look at the situation in Canada where aboriginal peoples are likewise worried about the crisis in indigenous languages. Comparisons with similar innovations such as the N'ungosuk of Manitoulin Island in Ontario reveal the likelihood of an uphill struggle in establishing the principles of aboriginal language immersion preschools.

Te Kohanga Reo: Organizing for Language Renewal

>Ko te reo te mauri o te tangata
>Ko te reo te mauri o te mana Maori

>Language is the essence of human existence.
>Language is the life principle of Maori vitality.

Historical Background: From Neglect to Resurgence
Prior to European contact in the late 18th century, the various tribes collectively known as the Maori comprised the aboriginal inhabitants (tangata whenua) of New Zealand (Aotearoa). Foraging and horticultural skills served to sustain a highly competitive society organized

tribally (iwi) around relatively self-sufficient villages (hapu) of extended families (whanau) (Metge 1976). But following sustained settlement by Europeans after 1840, the status of Maoridom began to decline. Consistent with public perception of Maoris as a "social problem" in need of solution, Maori cultural values were dismissed as irrelevant to New Zealand requirements.

Nowhere was this more evident than in the deterioration of Maori language as a system of communication. Pressures--from benign neglect to outright repression at schools--resulted in the restriction of Maori to private or ceremonial contexts (Dewes 1968, Barrington 1970). By the late 1970s, fluency in te reo Maori was confined generally to middle-aged rural dwellers. Maori youths were for the most part cut adrift from even tacit recognition of their language and cultural background (Benton 1979). To be sure, language assimilation was not total. Yet initiatives such as Maori Family Preschools, bilingual schools, and Maori language courses served only to accentuate the magnitude of the problem (McDonald 1976, Benton 1981). These programs failed to capitalize on the enormous plasticity of young children. Nor did they duplicate the natural context in which language learning occurred. The conclusion was obvious: apart from its symbolic and emotive properties (Biggs,1972), the viability of Maori as a system of daily communication was imperilled by the pressures of rapid urbanization and assimilation. Only massive intervention could possibly avert the inevitable demise and disappearance.

In response to this concern and drawing its inspiration from the Department's community-based development philosophy of Tu Tangata ('stand tall') (Fleras 1984), the first language nests appeared in 1982. Two years later, a total of 262 centres with an average enrolment of 16 children (Maori Affairs Report 1983) were in operation. Each language nest was supported by a paid supervisor, trainees from the Labour Department, and an extensive network of parents and elders. By March of 1988, the number of 'ahanau' centres had expanded to 521 with enrolments of nearly 11,000 or 25% of Maori preschool children (Department of Statistics, 1989). Future projections predict an enrolment of nearly 75% of all Maori preschool children (Government Review Report 1988). Matching this growth has been extensive state support, both in terms of government funding (in excess of $30 million over three years) as well as assistance from government departments such as Education, Social Welfare, Health, and Labour. On the basis of this unprecedented growth, it is evident the concept of Maori language immersion preschools as signalled the dawn of a new era in Maori self-determination.

Objectives and Goals: Language Renewal through Cultural Enhancement

The Kohanga Reo can be envisaged as a system of alternate education for preschool children which is predominantly Maori in content, objectives, and style (Reedy 1982). A community-based and culturally-sensitive approach to language education is employed in hopes of fostering a balanced (holistic) development within children. These objectives appeal to a wide cross-section of the New Zealand community, thereby ensuring a broadly-based support for the principle of language immersion preschools. Specific goals ('kaupapa") within this mandate include the following.

Promotion of te reo Maori is without doubt the most explicitly cited goal. The Kohanga Reo reflects a determination of the part of the Maori population to reassert the priority of te reo Maori not only as a language of everyday use but also as a springboard for cultural renewal. Contrary to popular belief, the program is not concerned exclusively with language mastery or demands for fluency on cue (see also Britsch-Devaney 1988). Rather the Kohanga Reo endeavours to improve language exposure through personal learning experiences in a self-directed fashion. Language goals are focused around basic vocabulary, simple sentence structures, and short conversational routines.

To foster this sense of pride in "things Maori," children in ages from birth to five are immersed in a Maori context. Ideally, there is a near total reliance on the use of Maori as a medium of instruction: children are spoken to in Maori, they are expected to respond in Maori, and daily activities are arranged to maximize exposure to te taha Maori (the Maori side). Parents too are encouraged to take advantage of the momentum by speaking in Maori outside the language nests. In some cases, they themselves have enroled in Maori language classes as part of a broader commitment to their children. Initial results are promising: depending in part on the nature of the home environment, many children by entry into primary school acquire an ability to speak and understand elementary Maori constructions and expressions (Maori Affairs Report 1983, McTagget 1986). More importantly, they emerge from the Kohanga Reo with a heightened sense of who they are and where they came from--a not altogether insignificant accomplishment in light of the battered self-image many Maori children carry around with them (Karetu and Waite 1989).

A secondary goal entails the promotion of and Maori cultural values. In view of the powerful relation between language and culture, proponents of the Kohanga Reo have stressed the cultural dimension of Maori language immersion preschools. A cultural environment is deliberately constructed whereby children are saturated with Maori knowledge, values, customs, and crafts.

This cultural dimension is also reflected in the actual location of these language nests, daily operation, activities and programs, and Maori styles of learning. Particularly salient to the operations are those familial values underlying traditional Maori methods of child rearing and socialization.

The Kohanga Reo vigorously endorses the centrality of an extended family network (shanau). The organizational framework is organized around the whanau in hopes of tapping into community resources and resourcefulness. The term whanau itself encompasses a broad set of referents with situationally specific meanings. In respect to the Kohanga Reo, whanau is employed in two meaningful senses: first, it conveys the idea of a traditional extended family arrangement wherein children were socialized in an environment surrounded by the presence of grandparents, relatives and other children (Metge 1976). Second, the concept of whanau maybe extended to include a cluster of values implicit within Maori domesticity. These include among others the virtues of aroha (caring, sharing and empathy), whanaungatanga (family responsibilities), rangimarie (peacefulness), and manaaki (kindness). In combining both applications, the image of a Kohanga Reo as a whanau centre is a powerful one which acknowledges the supportive role of the extended family within a rapidly changing urban context. A passage from the Department's handbook on the Kohanga Reo published in 1982 emphasizes this interdependence:

> The key to tKR is whanau. The tKR programme is designed to stimulate the growth of Maori whanau centres which can in turn offer the best environment possible for their children. It is a place where the Maori language will prevail and where love and care spring from the whanau. These centres can be in many places such as homes, maraes, churches, factories, offices, kokiri centres and the like. It is simply any place where the whanau Maori can operate with its natural and effective style.

In short, the Kohanga Reo program is made available through a network of whanau centres. The linking of Maoris under the whanau umbrella instills an ethos of community and collaboration for completion of the task at hand. As well, the whanau serves as the wellspring from which Maori children emerge with the skills and self-confidence for entry into either the Maori or non-Maori world.

The goal of compensatory education for Maori children is also implicit within the Kohanga Reo Authorities in New Zealand have long explored the potential of special programs for Maoris to offset the effects of perceived deficiencies in language and culture (Ritchie 1978, Bereiter and Englemann 1966, Child Care Services 1985, Teasdale and Whitelaw 1981). In the belief that Maori failure in schools originates from a poor self-image and a misplaced cultural identity (James 1988), the Kohanga Reo also stresses the development of social, verbal, and intellectual skills. Personal discipline, order, and respect for authority are taught alongside such acquired habits as paying attention, following instructions and learning to get along with others. Not everyone, however, concurs with this interpretation of Kohanga Reo as New Zealand's equivalent of 'Head Start'. Disagreement continues to be elicited over its focus as compensatory education ("preparation for school") or as an alternate expression of Maori learning ("preparation for life") (Fleras 1983, Douglas and Douglas 1983).

Structure and Operations: Community-Based and Culturally-Sensitive

A cultural dimension pervades the overall organization of the Kohanga Reo. Although aspects of conventional preschool system prevail our of necessity, these are drafted onto a framework which essentially is Maori in structure, operation, and style. The Kohanga Reo is in no position to tamper with certain regulations common to all preschool centres pertaining to nourishment, sanitation, and supervision. But beyond these requirements the Maori component is pervasive. most language nests, for example, are located at a Maori-owned premise such as a marae (Maori meeting place/ceremonial complex). With its antiquity, protocol, and rich symbolism, a marae-based environment is aptly suited as a venue for language exposure and stimulation.

Each language nest conforms to a basic daily routine which tends to bypass formal pedagogical approaches. Learning sessions are kept informal and consistent with Maori learning values. The emphasis in on language education through various repetitive actions in song, play and instruction (Metge 1984). Formal teaching methods are eschewed in favour of learning by exposure and verbal exchange between the child and adult. To provide the optimal conditions for language learning, most whanau centres cultivate as natural an environment as possible. Educational aids and equipment are generally downplayed in favour of resources inherent in the Maori social, cultural, or physical world. Even the introduction of sophisticated technology such as computers and video cassettes is retailored to meet whanau needs. Finally, a spiritual (wairua) dimension is strongly emphasized. Prayers (karakia) are conducted throughout the day to accentuate the inseparability of the spiritual and temporal element of Maoritanga.

The personnel of a language nest reflect a strong community component. They comprise paid supervisor(s), trainees from the Labour Department, and a voluntary sector of interested parents, grandparents and children. Also drawn into the partnership are officials from government bodies such as the Department of Maori Affairs, Education, and Health. All supervisors or kaitiaki (servant of the people) are selected on the strength of their Maori skills. Training is conducted under a Kohang Reo certificate program for licensing purposes (Kohanga Trust meeting 1984). The whanau training package consists of practical work experience (440 hours) and five modules (or 100 hours each) on Maori cultural concept. Relevant aspects of Maoritanga are stressed pertaining to (a) Maori wairua (spirituality, including myth and genealogy), (b) nga tikanga Maori (Maori concepts and celebrations), (c) te manaki tinana (Maori health and related customs), (d) te mita o te reo (Maori language skills and early childhood development), and (e) te whakahaere o nga kohanga reo (setting up and running a family-based preschool system). Control over the Kohanga Reo is likely to remain in Maori hands with the establishment of a whanau curriculum (Te Kohanga Reo Trust Certificate Syllabus 1983).

The partnership element is evident from levels of participation and input. Recruitment is focused around members of the local community whose resources and resourcefulness are pivotal in determining the outcome of individual language nests. Parents and grandparents are encouraged to become involved as part of their contribution toward the revival of te reo Maori. Some assume an active role in looking after children; others, however, prefer to serve in a back-up or supplementary fashion. Elders (kaumatua) are especially sought after as irreplaceable founts of knowledge and experience (see also Blondin 1989). This sustained interaction among parents, children and grandparents is perceived as critical in reconciling the intergeneration gap. It is also crucial in integrating the Kohanga Reo as living experience within the community at large.

Daily administrative work and long-term planning for each language nest belongs to a parent-controlled managing committee. In keeping with the whanau principle, this managing committee of locally recruited persons takes control over issues such as budgeting and programming. The role of the Maori Affairs Department is consistent with its Tu Tangata philosophy of community-based development in tandem with government support. The government transfers some resources and expertise, primarily in the form of "seeding grants" and temporary labour trainees. Interference from central authorities is kept to a minimum, although Departmental community officers are expected to maintain a degree of contact. Each language nest is thus structured around a line of development consistent with community strengths, not bureaucratic imperatives. To assist in coordination and promotion at national levels, a Kohanga Reo Trust Body has been instituted of select Maori authorities and community leaders. This body is responsible for monitoring and shaping overall growth, but not to the point of undermining the relative autonomy--or credibility--of each language nest. The Trust also acts on behalf of the program in making submissions to the government and state agencies for financial support and political legitimacy.

Summing up: Preschooling With a Cultural Difference

The Kohanga Reo stands at the forefront of a Maori cultural rejuvenation with language renewal as a key component in the revitalizing process (James 1988). The community-based and culturally-sensitive dimensions of the Kohanga Reo are clearly delineated around the principle of Maori control over Maori language education. In reasserting the primacy of selected Maori customs-particularly those based on obligations to kin (Fitzgerald 1977)--the Kohanga Reo reinforces the value of traditional networks and community-based partnership for Maori achievement. Promotion of this Maori dimension accentuates the distinctiveness of the Kohanga Reo as "preschooling with a cultural difference."

The Sharp End of the Stick: The Impact of the Kohanga Reo

The Kohanga Reo is arguably the central dynamic in redefining Maori-non-Maori relations in New Zealand. The impact of the Kohanga Reo in promoting Maori political and cultural aspirations cannot be taken lightly. It represents the most visible manifestation of this resurgent interest in Maori language against the backdrop of Maori self-determination as tangata whenua. As a catalyst for social change, the Kohanga Reo has focused a critical mass of attention of the Maori language crisis, united disparate Maori elements into actions, and created conditions favourable for political reform. Much of its success can be attributed to the fusion of Maori cultural values with a traditional learning base. Maori cultural values are no longer dismissed as irrelevant to an urban environment or inimical to social progress. Under Kohanga Reo, they are espoused as synonymous with Maori advancement in partnership with central authorities. This passage taken from a Maori Affairs report acknowledges as much:

> The particular problems facing many Maori families and their children in today's world are well understood. The difficulty has been to find appropriate systems that could tap into the depth of resources and expertise of the Maori communities themselves. In the last five years we have seen a tremendous surge in confidence and action from the Maori people, particularly within the umbrella of the Tu Tangata philosophy, which has produces such successful ventures as Kokiri and Kohanga Reo -programmes that concentrate very much on child care and youth development. A key strength that has emerged from these Maori social changes is the positioning today of strong whanau groups with a capability to administer even more sophisticate social and cultural programs (Maatua Whangai Policy Report 1983)

The Kohanga Reo is strategically located to harness the enthusiasm, commitment, and participation of the community. The program operates within a Maori social and cultural framework, thus allowing a wide array of Maori opinion and input. This openness to community and culture reinforces the concept of Kohanga Reo as a Maori response to meet Maori needs in a Maori way. In the words of Kathie Cameron (1984: 51):

> This is what Kohanga Reo are all about. They are total school environments which are Maori--they have Maori curriculum, counselling techniques, parental involvement, teaching styles, learning styles, whanau organisation. All variables in the education environment reflect a Maori perspective. And Kohanga Reo are successful.

The Maori community also derives benefits from the presence of the Kohanga Reo. Once established, the language nests themselves become centres of community interest and activity, a focus for Maori cultural and language survival, a basis for related community projects in education or development, and adaptive mechanisms for traditional strengths to meet contemporary needs (see also Department of Statistics 1989). The creation of a community focal point is especially important for young mothers who might otherwise feel alienated and isolated in coping with the demands of urban society. A respected Maori elder has claimed:

> It is a common fact that the urban scene becomes a nightmare for the solo parent. Hence you have a situation in many cities where young mothers are imprisoned in the impersonal and lonely constraints of the concrete jungle. That they never even get to meet other women of the same situation or older women who may add another dimension to their lives is an accepted fact. What we now have with the rise of TKR are situations where women can meet each other in a child care situation, a whanau situation and very often a cultural situation. So immediately you place TKR in the midst of the impersonal cold concrete city, suddenly you have a changed situation. (John Rangihau 1984).

No less significant is the potential to mobilize the Maori communities. Parental involvement has resulted not only in a collective and individual empowerment, but also a growing politicization of grassroot's activism. A case in point: Maori parents (especially women) have begun to question the role and functions of the education system, in the process acquiring the skills and commitment for collective protest action.

The impact of the Kohanga Reo is equally noticeable outside the Maori Realm. By virtue of its success the Kohanga Reo has challenged the existing preschool organization to incorporate Maori needs aspirations (Report, Nga Tumanako, 1984; also Smith, 1983). The Education Department also has urged closer links with the Kohanga Reo on the grounds of mutual cultural interests:

> The Department welcomes kohanga reo and will continue to work closely with the Department of Maori Affairs and the Maori people in their further developments. Their aims and objectives are those the Department has been seeking to achieve through its policies over the years: to increase the use of Maori, to make Maori language and culture accessible to all children whose parents wish them to learn it; to assist in preserving Maori language and culture; and to promote cross-cultural understanding (New Zealand Education Gazette 1984).

Lastly, it is difficult to ignore the penetration of the Kohanga Reo in shaping Maori-government relations. Impressed by the popularity of

Kohanga Reo as the "thin wedge" of a Maori groundswell, the Labour government passed legislation in 1987 to make Maori an official language of New Zealand (in courts and Parliament), has applied the partnership principles implicit within the Treaty of Waitangi across a wide range of government legislation, has expended on the jurisdiction of the Waitangi Tribunal to include post-1840 Maori grievances for redress, has instructed all government departments to incorporate a Maori perspective (te taha Maori); and has initiated moves to decentralize and devolve state structures in line with partnership perspectives (Fleras 1989). This has become particularly noticeable following moves by the government to channel resources, administration, developmental projects, and communication through Maori tribal (iwi) organizations (Labour Government 1988). With the recent phasing out of the Maori Affairs Department, tribal authorities are likely emerge as key performers in forging a bicultural New Zealand (Dyall 1988, Fleras 1989).

In sum, the impact of the Kohonga Reo on Maori and non-Maori sectors has been widespread. A growing number of Maori children are now capable of speaking (or at least identifying with) te reo Maori. Numerous parents have acquired renewed confidence and a sense of empowerment in their ability to advance Maori cultural interests. The New Zealand government has actively courted the Kohanga Reo in renewing its links with an increasingly assertive Maori Community. For Maori activists, the Kohanga Reo has evolved into a powerful symbol of protest for spearheading Maori aboriginal interest. In short, by imparting a tangible expression to Maori demands, the Kohanga Reo has indeed emerged as the "sharp end of the stick" in redefining Maori-government relations (Fleras 1987a, 1987b).

Canadian Aboriginal Language Education: Problems and Prospects

> If our peoples' languages are to survive and to experience the resurgence which is necessary for survival, we must act immediately and must develop resources, skills, and understanding of what is necessary on a community-based level. Only then, in my opinion, will there be some assurance that our aboriginal languages continue as a living force, thereby enabling our peoples' cultural strengths to continue to grow and flourish.
> (Verna Kirkness, Director of the First Nations House of Learning, University of British Columbia.)

Native Canadian Indians like their counterparts in New Zealand have displayed a growing concern over the status of aboriginal languages (Shkilnyk 1985). The parallels are striking. Notwithstanding increased exposure to native language instruction both on and off the reserve, most Native Indian languages are rapidly approaching a critical stage (Price 1981, Shkilynk 1986). Fluent native speakers are disappearing as increased numbers of youth turn to English as the preferred language of communication at home and in public Canadian Native Indians Report 1984). Even in relatively remote areas--such as Manitoulin Island in Ontario--the crisis in aboriginal languages is apparent.

Native leaders are now taking corrective action in the teeth of assimilationist pressures to undermine the linguistic basis of aboriginal identity (Burnaby 1982, 1984). Band-operated and cultural-survival schools have proliferated in an effort to exercise parental responsibility and community control (Barman, Hebert, and McCaskill 1987, McCaskill 1987). Bilingual programming where native languages are employed as the language of instruction has grown in popularity throughout Canada (Frideres 1988). Yet tinkering with modifications to the curriculum may be ineffective for native language fluency (Shkilnyk 1985; Barman, Hebert, and McCaskill 1987). By way of reaction to cosmetic reforms, some have argued that nothing short of partial or total immersion can reverse the tide. Aboriginal language immersion programs have been proposed at the primary level--notably among the Six Nation Cayuga (Toronto Star, 19 August, 1986) and at Kahnawake Reserve near Montreal (Toronto Star, 16 February, 1987). But with few exceptions (Canadian Education Association 1984: 79), the concept of language immersion at the preschool level has not attracted much attention or enthusiasm.

The Solution: N'ungosuk as Ojibwa Language Immersion Preschool

N'ungosuk represents an Ojibwas language immersion preschool which originated in 1982 among West Bay residents on Manitoulin Island (Hall 1986). Established by a small circle of dedicated parents, N'ungosuk has not achieved a high level of community involvement despite widespread support for the principle of Indian control over Indian education. Rather N'ungosuk has drawn its vitality from a small number of dedicated persons with a commitment to sustain a native language environment. Enrolment at N'ungosuk has averaged around 15-20 children between the ages of two and five. Emphasis is on a holistic development (education as a total way of life) of the children's intellectual, spiritual, and cultural aspects. The operation itself is conducted out of an apartment complex designed primarily for single mothers. Personnel are comprised of paid staff (supervisors), volunteers, and (grand)parents, in addition to relative and friends who act as resource and instructional personnel. Elders are eagerly sought after to impart some element of continuity in addition to credibility to the project.

The Kohanga Reo and N'ungosuk share similarities in terms of objectives, organization, and style. The N'ungosuk begins with the assumption that the most influential methods of language renewal are conducted within a community-based setting, utilize the native tongue as the language of instruction, and are directed by immersion toward children at the formative stages of language development. They are spoken to in Ojibwa, and are expected to respond accordingly although there is no punishment for English usage. Ojibwa is employed exclusively as the vehicle of verbal communication throughout the daily routine of supervised play and formal instruction. The results of this immersion appear to be impressive. Preschoolers have acquired a familiarity with Ojibwa language and culture and appear anxious to convey their competence to others (Hall 1986).

Perils and Pitfalls in Aboriginal Language Preschooling

As noted, N'ungosuk resembles the Kohanga Reo in many respect. Both ultimately are concerned with the preservation of a threatened language base by means of community-based actions. Yet differences in impact are glaring. One has flourished and prospered beyond all expectations, while the other languishes in relative obscurity. In contrast with the Kohanga Reo, the N'ungosuk has encountered numerous problems in promoting itself as a legitimate expression of aboriginal preschool education. Foremost is the failure to achieve widespread community consensus. Unlike the situation in New Zealand where parental involvement and community contributions are overwhelming, many Ojibwas parents have withheld support for fear of interfering with the development of English speaking skills. Several key principles of community development can be identified as central to the success of such an enterprise (see Fleras 1984, Minister of Corrections and Services 1989). These include, first, a bottom-up approach in the planning, delivery, and evaluation of local language nests; second, the centrality of the community context as it related to local Maori customs, values, needs, and concerns; third, a certain degree of flexibility, access, and responsiveness to local input inherent in each language nest; fourth, widespread involvement of all community members, with particular emphasis on elders; fifth, abiding faith in the community as a source of strength and resources; and sixth, provision of adequate government resources to allow each community to identify the issues and problems, to develop appropriate lines of action for addressing these concerns, and implement plans for change consistent with local structures, priorities, and cultural values (see Hansen 1987). This combination of community--orientation and cultural--sensitivity reflects what is widely regarded as a Maori style of doing things. It also reinforces an identification with Maori cultural values as integral and relevant components of a Maori renewal.

Secondly, the two programs differ in the degree and scope of external support. Except for start-up financing, the N'ungosuk has not received much in the way of government funding. Although the Department of Education and of Indian Affairs acknowledge the crisis in aboriginal languages, they appear reluctant to support N'ungosuk on fiscal, political, or jurisdictional grounds (Fleras 1987a). Federal commitment to French and English bilingualism leaves aboriginal immersion programs with little room to manoeuvre--at least until the time when aboriginal languages are accorded a formal status within the framework of aboriginal rights (see Hall 1986). Given this lack of community receptivity and political will, the N'ungosuk cannot hope to match the levels of success attained by the Kohanga Reo.

Conclusion and Summary: Language as Power, Power as Language

Our native language embodies a value system about how we ought to live and relate to each other... it gives a name to relations among kin, to roles and responsibilities among family members, to ties with the broader clan group...There are no English works for these relationships because your social and family life is different from ours. Now if you destroy our language, you not only break down these relationships, but you also destroy other aspects of our Indian way of life and culture, especial those that describe man's connection with nature, the Great Spirit, the order of things. Without our language, we will cease to exist as a separate people
(Eli Taylor, Dakota-Sioux from Manitoba, quoted in Shkilnyk 1985).

Debate over language issues has emerged recently at the cutting edge of minority efforts to restructure the relationships of power in society (Taylor and Giles 1979, Dramarae 1984, Fleras 1987b). This is especially true among aboriginal sectors whose language is regarded as a highly visible manifestation of people's aspirations, selfhood, and world view (Kennedy 1983, Sutcliffe 1986). Not only are aboriginal languages perceived as the embodiment of cultural distinctiveness and identity, their preservation is also upheld as a rallying point to mobilize, advance, and legitimize aboriginal activism (see Ross 1979). By rephrasing the language crisis in terms of aboriginal self-determination rather than as a problem of communication preference, the often abstract demands of aboriginality are compressed and conveyed in a manner acceptable to central policy structures (Fleras 1987b).

Consistent with this notion of language-as-power and power-as-language, the Kohanga Reo in New Zealand has explored the possibility of language preservation through total immersion at the preschool level. It has also reinforced the necessity for culturally-unique and community-based development as a starting point in linking government support with local involvement. The social impact and policy implications have been nothing short of startling: the Kohanga Reo has resulted in (a) the politicization of aboriginal issues in a relatively unthreatening manner; (b) the legitimation of aboriginal claims as valid and necessary in a bicultural society; (c) the presentation of aboriginal demands on terms that central policy structures can relate to; and (d) the mobilization of the Maori public around the principle of Maori self-determination.

Similarly, Canadian Native Indian have also taken steps to renew aboriginal language rights. Different strategies for renewal have been employed, but with mixed results. Yet a proposal to employ a system of native language immersion preschools--like those of the Kohanga Reo--has failed to garner political or community support. Failure to politicize the aboriginal language crisis or to engage in issue-linkage has been partly responsible. That being the case, until broader issues pertaining to aboriginal self-government are constitutionally resolved, the crisis in aboriginal language education will persist.

References

Awatere, Donna (1984).
　Maori Sovereignty. Auckland: Broadsheets.
Barman, J., Hebert, Y., and McCaskill, D. (eds.) (1987).
　Indian Education in Canada: The Challenge. Vancouver: University of British Columbia Press.
Barrington, J. M. (1970).
　A Historical Review of Policies and Provisions. In J. L. Ewing and J. S. Shallcrass (eds.), Introduction to Maori Education: Selected Readings., 27-39. Wellington: New Zealand University Press.
Benton, Richard A. (1979).
　Who Speaks Maori in New Zealand? Wellington: New Zealand Council of Educational Research.
Benton, Richard A. (1981).
　The Flight of the Amokura. Wellington: New Zealand Council of Educational Research.
Bereiter, C. and Englemann, S. (1966)
　Teaching Disadvantaged Children in the Preschool. Englewood Cliffs: Prentice-Hall.
Biggs, Bruce (1972).
　The Maori Language Past and Present. In Erik Schwimmer (ed.), The Maori People in the Nineteen Sixties, 65-84. Auckland: Longman Paul.
Blondin, Georgina (1989).
　The Development of the Zhahti Koe Slavey Language Program. Canadian Journal of Native Education 16: 89-106.
Britsch-Devany, Susan (1988).
　The Collaborative Development of a Language Renewal Program for Preschoolers. Human Organization 47: 297-301.
Burnaby, Barbara (1982).
　Language and Education among Canadian Native Peoples. Toronto: OISE Press.
Burnaby, Barbara (1984).
　Aboriginal Languages in Ontario. Toronto: Ministry of Education.
Cameron, Kathie (1984).
　Responding to the Challenge of Multicultural Education. Delta 34: 45-53.
Canadian Education Association (1984).
　Recent Developments in Native Education. Toronto: Canadian Education Association.

Department of Statistics (1989).
 The New Zealand Official Yearbook. Wellington.
Dewes, Koro. (1968).
 The Place of Maori Language in the Education of the Maoris. Paper presented to the 40th ANZAAS Congress at Christchurch, New Zealand.
Douglas, E. M. K. and Douglas, R. B. (1983).
 Nga Kohanga Reo: A Salvage Programmer for the Maori Language. Paper presented to the 53 ANZAAS Congress at Perth Australia.
Dyall, Lorna. (1988).
 He Tirohanga Rangapu. Partnership Perspective. A Discussion Paper. Public Sector 11: 9-11.
Dyck, Noel (ed.) (1985).
 Indigenous Peoples and the Nation-State. Fourth World Politics in Canada, Australia, and Norway. St. Johns: Memorial University.
Edwards, Jonathan (1985).
 Language, Society, and Identity. London: Basil Blackwell.
Fitzgerald, Thomas K. (1977).
 Education and Identity. A Study of the New Zealand Maori Graduate. Wellington: New Zealand Council of Educational Research.
Fleras, A. J. (1983).
 Te Kohanga Reo: Preparation for Life or Preparation for School? Published Report on Maori Language Preschools, Maori Affairs Department, Wellington.
Fleras, A. J. (1985).
 Towards "Tu Tangata": Historical Developments and Current Trends in Maori Policy and Administration. Political Science 37: 18-39.
Fleras, A. J. (1987a).
 Redefining the Politics over Aboriginal Language Renewal: Maori Language Preschools as Agents of Social Change. The Canadian Journal of Native Studies 7: 1-40.
Fleras, A. J. (1987b).
 Aboriginality as a Language Issue: The Politicization of te reo Maori in New Zealand. Plural Societies 17: 25-51.
Fleras, A. J. (1989).
 Inverting the Bureaucratic Pyramid: Debureaucratizing the Maori Affairs Department in New Zealand. Human Organization 48: 214-225.

Frideres, James (1988).
   Native Peoples in Canada. Contemporary Conflicts. Englewood Cliffs: Prentice-Hall.
Greenland, Hauraki (1984).
   Ethnicity as Ideology. The Critique of Pakeha Society. In Paul Spoonley et al. (eds.), Tauiwi: Racism and Ethnicity in New Zealand., 86-102. Palmerston North: Dunmore Press.
Hall, Anthony J. (1986).
   The N'ungosuk Project. A Study in Aboriginal Language Renewal. Unpublished Paper.
Hansen, Barbara (1987).
   Community Development. Unpublished Paper.
James, Colin (1988).
   New Zealand Maori Challenge. Far Eastern Economic Review 141: 36-42.
Karetu, Timoti and Waite, Jeffrey. (1989).
   Te Reo Maori. New Zealand Yearbook, 217-227. Wellington: Government Printer.
Kennedy, Chris (ed.). (1983).
   Language Planning and Language Education. London: George Allen and Unwin.
Kramarae, Cheris (1984).
   Introduction: Toward an Understanding of Language and Power. In Cheris Kramarae et al. (eds.), Language and Power. 9-22. Beverley Hills: Sage Publications.
Little Bear, Leroy, Boldt, Menno, and Long, A. J. (1984).
   Pathways to Self-Determination. Canadian Indians and the Canadian State. Toronto: University of Toronto Press.
McCaskill, Don. (1987).
   Revitalization of Indian Culture: Indian Cultural Survival Schools. In Jean Barman et al. (eds.), Indian Education in Canada: The Challenge, 153-179. Vancouver: University of British Columbia Press.
McDonald, Geraldine (1973).
   Maori Mothers and Pre-school Education. Wellington: New Zealand Council of Educational Research.
McTagget, Sue. (1986).
   Leaving the Nest. Listener (NZ), November 22.
Metge A. Joan (1976).
   The Maoris of New Zealand. London: Routledge and Kegan Paul.
Ministry of Community and Social Services (1989).
   Better Beginnings, Better Futures. An Integrated Mode of Primary Prevention of Emotional and Behavioural Disorders. Toronto: Queens Printer.

Orange, Claudia (1987).
   The Treaty of Waitangi. Wellington: Allen and Unwin.
Paine, Robert (1985).
   The Claims of the Fourth World. In Jens Brosted (ed.), The Quest for Autonomy and Nationhood of Indigenous Peoples, 49-66. Bergen: Universitetforlaget.
Price, John (1981).
   The Viability of Indian Languages in Canada. Canadian Journal of Native Studies 1: 339-346.
Puketapu, Kara (1982). Reform From Within. Paper presented to a Public Service Management Group, Wellington.
Reedy, Tamati (1982). Fostering the Growth of Indigenous Languages. Paper presented to the Second Indigenous Peoples International Conference at Honolulu.
Rice, Vernon and James, Colin. (1987).
   Old Treaty Given Maori Cultural Renaissance a Political Dimension. International Herald Tribune, December 1.
Ritchie, Jane (1978).
   Chance to be Equal. Whakamongo Bay, New Zealand: Cape Catly.
Ross, J. A. (1979).
   Language and the Mobilization of Ethnic Identity. In H. Giles and B. St.-Jacques (eds.), Language and Ethnic Relations, 1-14. Oxford: Pergamon Press.
Shkilnyk, Anastasia M. (1985).
   Canada's Aboriginal Languages: An Overview of Current Activities in Language Retention. Unpublished Report for the Secretary of State.
Smith, N. G. H. (1983).
   The School's Role in Relation to the Te Kohanga Reo Child, Unpublished Discussion Paper.
Stea, David and Wisner, Ben (1984).
   The Fourth World. A Geography of Indigenous Struggles. Antipodes 16: 3-12.
Sutcliffe, David (1986).
   Introduction. In David Sutcliffe and Ansel Wong (eds.). The Language of Black Experience, 1-14. Oxford: Basil Blackwell.
Tastily, G. R. and Whitely, A. J. (1981).
   The Early Childhood Education of Aboriginal Australians. A Review of Six Action-Research Projects. Victoria: ACER.
Taylor, D. M. and Giles, H. (1979).
   At the Crossroads of Research into Language and Ethnic Relations. In H. Giles and B. St.-Jacques (eds.) Language and Ethnic Relations, 231-241. Oxford: Pergammon Press.

INDIAN EDUCATION: AN ALTERNATIVE PROGRAM

by
J.S. Frideres and W.J. Reeves
The University of Calgary

Introduction

The present paper begins with a brief overview of the Canadian educational system and how Indians fit into the school system, and concludes with an outline of a program for integrating Indians into post-secondary educational institutions. This program would alleviate some of the problems currently facing both students and instructors.

There has been an expansion of education, including higher education, world wide. National systems of education have been extended to incorporate an ever increasing proportion of the population (Meyer et al, 1977; Craig, 1981). There is international acknowledgement that education is an integral component of economic and national development (Ramierez and Boli, 1982; Lewin et al, 1982). Educational qualifications increasingly have a bearing on a person's ability to secure a position with leadership potential in the large corporations, public and private, that dominate key sectors of our society (Collins, 1979). More generally, educational qualifications increasingly have a bearing upon the ability to negotiate and conduct business both public and private, with these dominant organizations (Fiala and Lanford, 1987).

The education system provides a predictable, often age-graded series of sequences that shape the life course experienced by an increasing proportion of the population. Elementary and high school are followed by four years of undergraduate studies, and two or more years of graduate or professional education. Those able to make the transition into an organizational or occupational career ladder continue to experience sequenced structuring of important opportunities. Members of the public who remain "on-track" display high levels of personal efficacy, self- control and self-esteem, attributes we associate with competence and success. Marginal "off-track" groups in society; school dropouts, women outside the labour force, the unemployed, and Native people do not display these qualities.

The greater the proportion of the population entering education-based sequenced opportunity structures, the more pronounced the discontinuity experienced by those who find themselves off-track and excluded. The psychological reaction to exclusion from these sociologically significant structures tends to produce a self-fulfilling cycle of action and reaction that may be termed a status disability. The mobilization of a greater proportion of the population into secondary and especially higher levels of education that we associate with development tends to heighten the status disability experienced by the excluded and dispossessed.

Status disabilities violate our society's notions of natural justice and equality. Political and cultural demands for remedy are highly legitimate. Individuals experiencing status disabilities raise issues that command public attention and professional groups and social movements emerge, championing the cause of those afflicted. These advocates identify sociological circumstances and psychological symptoms as dimensions of a social problem that requires social action (Meyer, 1987).

Canadian Educational System

At the turn of the century, Canada was an agricultural economy and, as such, few individuals received extensive formal academic education. Katz (1970) points out that in the mid-1800s, advanced education was only for a small number who attended grammar schools, colleges, and/ or universities. Young people sporadically attended school, left before completing the program, and were generally of upper-middle class background. While some costs were borne by the government, most of the financial burden was placed on the parents or on the individual student. However, by the late nineteenth century, education began to be viewed by a larger segment of the Canadian society as a means of achieving upward mobility as well as a method of achieving national unity and political stability (Synge, 1976).

As the twentieth century began, new conceptualizations of/regarding education emerged. Education, in addition to training people, now

was believed to alleviate social problems of the time. It was at this time that the philosophy of "democratic goals" was inculcated into the curriculum of Canadian education. These educational philosophies included the following:
(i) provide all children, regardless of social attributes, with equivalent opportunities for self-development and educational and occupational advancement.
(ii) efforts should be made to provide advanced education to those who merit it.
(iii) education would be the major process of immigrant assimilation.

It is the third aspect of the "educational ideology"[1] that is most germane to Native People. Assimilation refers to the social process through which culturally and social diverse groups become fused together into one social unit with a common culture (Vander Zanden, 1965; Gordon, 1964). While assimilation was the official pronouncement of school ideology, the definition provided above was not what *school officials* meant by it. Their definition was what academics now call "Anglo conformity;" the ideology of maintaining English institutions, language and culture and forcing all other groups to take on the dominant culture[2].

Acculturation and assimilation were expected to produce a monocultural society. This could be accomplished depending upon how closely various ethnic groups approximated the dominant group -- British[3]. This ideology accepted the idea that some groups were so different that it would be impossible to assimilate them into Canadian society. Native people throughout the history of Canada have been at the edges of such a definition.

Nevertheless, assimilation into Canadian society through the process of education continues to be an important theme in the ideology of contemporary school systems, although developments over the past two decades in our society have led, to some degree, to the incorporation of cultural pluralism into our school system. While the philosophy of cultural pluralism is not new, until recently it was not implemented by the school system. Schools have consistently tried to instill homogeneous values and attitudes in children by teaching them that one way (the dominant mode) of doing things is superior to all others, rather than teaching children to value cultural differences and to respect those of different backgrounds and beliefs.

By the 1950s the ideology of the school system was being challenged. (Tamminga, 1977). Confrontations between school officials, ethnic minority parents and minority communities began to occur with increasing frequency. The relationship between education, poverty, social equality and school programs began to assume increased political significance. Local and national politicians, professional educations, and school administrators were forced to respond to the new demands for equal educational opportunity. Minority groups began, to the surprise of educators, to argue that differential rates of educational achievement and school failure *were not* a function of ethnic group characteristics but rather the structure of the educational system.

Ethnic identity became an important issue in the confrontation between the schools and minority communities. Minority groups pressed for curriculum reforms, including minority history and ethnic studies, and asked that education be made relevant for minority children; that it contribute to positive self-images and ethnic pride. While changes in attitudes toward ethnic and cultural diversity have occurred recently, there still exists resistance to the ideology of cultural pluralism in the schools.

Urban school systems are formal organizations, oriented to the production of output that constitutes input for other social systems. Hence, the school provides the individual with an "education" that is to be utilized by the economic, political and other institutional orders. Two kinds of education are produced: instrumental and expressive. Instrumental education is the acquisition of information and skills necessary for enacting specified technical roles. Hence, the curriculum will focus on certain substantive subject matter and provide incentives for student performance. Expressive education is the development of beliefs and various forms of sensibility. Instrumental education thus became a means for social understanding and mobility. School systems also emphasize expressive goals such as thrift, cleanliness, punctuality, and honesty,[4] which are related to social mobility.

During the 1960s, educational researchers began to support those arguments of the minority community. Schools were not effective in breaking the poverty cycle and eliminating racial discrimination. Minority leaders and certain educators urged that schools compensate for social disadvantages of the poor as well as the differences experienced by ethnic groups. Hence, groups rather than individuals, became the focus of their definition of what constituted equality of opportunity. As Church (1976) points out, these people argued that schools served the interests of equality and democracy only when they succeeded in teaching all their citizens the skills necessary to live in and compete in the modern world. This argument did not reject the notion of competition or meritocracy. Rather, it is argued that these processes be postponed to the "post" schools years. It was also during this period that research began to point to a relationship between pupils' self-concept and school performance. Schools were placed under further pressure to improve student achievement by creating positive identities for ethnic minorities.

The early ethnic programs focussed on the expressive component of education which promoted specific ethnic identity and sense of individual worth. In the past, students and teachers were rewarded for conforming to White English middle-class norms. Today teachers are rewarded for enhancement of the self-concepts of students. Changes in the curriculum were necessary to increase its relevance and appeal to various ethnic groups since the content of the curriculum represents school goals and norms in practice (Cave and Cheslev, 1974). The new curriculum was expected to foster ethnic group pride and awareness and to present multi-ethnic perspectives on social and historical events in place of the singular Anglo perspective of the past.

Indian Education

From the time of the Royal Proclamation in 1763 to 1830, Indian education was under control of the military. By the mid-1800s, some arrangements were being made by the state for the provision of education for Natives. For example, in 1857 legislation was passed enabling municipalities in both Upper and Lower Canada with the following provision (Davey, 1965):
... on application of the Superintendent General of Indian Affairs, to attach the whole or any portion of any Indian reserves in such municipality, to a neighbouring school section or district, and such land shall thereupon become a portion of the school section or district to which it may be attached, to all intents and purposes (p.1).

A significant feature of government policy after Confederation was the completion of a series of treaties with Indians. In return for Indians surrendering their land, the government agreed, in one way or another, to make provision for Indian education. For example, Treaty #6 states: And further, Her Majesty agrees to maintain schools for instruction in such reserves hereby made, as to Her Government of the Dominion for Canada may seem advisable, whenever the Indians of the reserve shall desire it.

From confederation until World War II, it was assumed that Indians would remain on the reserves and thus the implementation of an education program extending beyond agricultural skills for Indians was unnecessary (Hawthorn, 1966-67). Social consciousness after World War II brought an increased awareness of the need for education for Native People. As O'Neill (1965) points out, the Joint Committee of Senate and House of Commons established in 1946

... hastened developments which led to the long overdue Act in 1951 and to provisions for the extension of educational programs downward to kindergarten and upward to secondary and university levels (p. 88).

This short history of Native education reveals the fact that prior to World War II, minimal education was provided to Native people and that was provided under the auspices of religious organizations. Religious residential schools were the major vehicle for carrying out the educational process. Until the social revolution of the mid-fifties, day schools were established on the reserves. In 1950, the federal government began systematically eliminating day schools on the reserves. By 1971, secondary schools on the reserve were virtually nonexistent. However, in the past decade, this process had been reversed with the number of on-reserve schools offering secondary education increasing from zero to 80. During this period, the total number of students in secondary schools on the reserve rose to over fourteen thousand.

The provisions of elementary and secondary educational services and finances for Natives derives it authority from section 114 to 119 and 121 to 123 of the Indian Act as well as by specific Orders in Council. Through their activities, Indian Affairs provides for educational services for approximately eighty thousand elementary/secondary students. These services are provided under three different conditions: federal, band and provincial. Currently, there are 162 federal and 219 band schools. Band schools are federally funded schools but are locally controlled and operated by Native people. The remainder of students are educated in provincial schools under 600 joint Federal-Provincial agreements.[5] These are regular provincial schools which agree to provide educational services for Natives on behalf of the federal government (see table 1).

Table 1
Student Enrollment by Type of School, 1978-1985

	78-79	79-80	80-81	81-82	82-83	83-84	84-85
Provincial	45,000	46,000	48,000	44,500	39,000	38,500	40,000
Federal	28,000	27,000	26,000	22,000	22,000	22,500	22,000
Band	6,000	7,500	9,000	11,500	16,500	17,500	18,000
TOTAL	79,500	80,500	83,000	78,000	77,500	78,500	80,000

Of these eighty thousand students, half received instruction in provincial schools while twenty-eight percent are educated in the federally operated schools.[6]

The formal educational achievements of Native people in Canada is considerably less than the non-Native population. Over fifteen percent of Natives of 15 years of age have less than a grade five education. Forty percent never went to high school (as opposed to 20 percent non-natives). While half of the general Canadian population have at least a high school diploma, less than one-quarter of the Natives hold one. About 28 percent of all Indians have a secondary education or more compared to 56 percent of all Canadians. Finally, nearly ten percent of the non-Native population have university degrees while less than 2 percent of Natives have such educational attainments (see table 2).

Table 2
Percent of Natives by Highest Level of Schooling
Native and Non-Native Population, 1981

	Native	Non-Native
Less than Grade 8	27.3	11.6
Less than Grade 9	41.0	22.6
Some high school	32.1	25.2
High School Diploma	6.1	13.4
Trade Certificate	2.4	3.7
At least some Post-Secondary	18.4	35.7

The retention rate for Indian students from grade two to 12/13 has increased from 18 percent (1975) to over thirty percent in 1984-85. Nearly 19 percent of Natives eighteen years and older had attained at least some post-secondary education in 1981 while a decade previous, less than three percent had done so. These figures show that Natives, at least at the elementary and secondary levels, are remaining in school longer. At the post-secondary level, over eight thousand Native students are enrolled.

This increase in elementary and secondary school attendance and achievement is partially a result of making the curriculum more relevant to Indians; the hiring of Indian teachers, aides and elders and, in some cases, the use of Indian languages in the classroom (in some cases, used as the language of instruction). The involvement of parents in the education of their children has also led to a greater participation in the educational institutions. Nevertheless, the current approach to Native education is universalistic in perspective. All students (Native and non-Native) are treated the same. Despite the Indians' extensive class and cultural diversity, they are treated similar to non-Native students.

Language and Education

There are fifty-three distinct indigenous languages spoken today (Hebert, 1984). Of the eleven major Native languages,[7] Algonquian is the largest with over 200,000 individuals having this as their ancestral language. Other Amerindian languages have much smaller language families, e.g., Athapaskan (30,000), Iroquaian (27,000), Salishan (25,000) and Eskimo-Alert (24,000). The remaining language groups even have smaller numbers; somewhere between 500 and less than ten thousand -- Wakashan, Tsimshian, Sioux, Haida, Tlinget and Kutenaian (Burnaby, 1982). Figures from the 1981 census show that Native people are increasingly becoming bilingual but are doing so without creating any transitional languages; they take English/French as their first or second language. Overall, less than fifty percent of on-reserve Indians have an Aboriginal language as their mother tongue. Variations in this pattern are evident. For example, seventy percent of Indians in Quebec have a Native mother tongue while only 15 percent in British Columbia. Of those who have a Native mother tongue, over three-fourths claim that they use it at home as an everyday language. This suggests that many Native people (particularly older Natives) still retain and use their Native language.

Notwithstanding the above, we also find that less than one-fourth of all Native students entering school are monolingual in an Amerindian language. An additional one-third are bilingual while the remaining 42 percent have English as their mother tongue with no working knowledge of a Native language. Additional data reveals that students with only Native languages are limited to isolated communities.

What impact does language have in the education of students? Native people have long argued that instruction in the Native mother tongue of young students is a necessity. They argue that a positive identity, high self-esteem and achievement in the school are all related to language of instruction. Toike (1987) and Cummins (1981) conclude that school adjustment, language, reading and the learning of other subject material by minority children are much better in a system where children are exposed to a good bilingual program rather than experience a majority language only program. Research suggests that elementary education presented in the mother tongue of the student will allow the student to understand the material easier and faster than if it is not presented in the student's mother tongue. After grade six, the medium of instruction may be switched over to a second language and the student will be able to transfer his/her skills. Nowhere, however, have Native languages been used in the formal education of Native children (Whyte, 1986). In addition, so few schools have Amerindian language programs that it is difficult to assess their impact. Furthermore, those few schools which have Native language programs also have extensive parental and community support which may have an impact on student achievement.[8] Generally the student attending school is subjected to a submersion approach in which the student is forced to take on English/French and give up his/her mother tongue. Hebert (1984) concludes her assessment of language programs in the school by arguing that if language acquisition and retention is the goal for Native people, then the home and community must become the real basis and location of language rention efforts.

Native language competence at the post secondary level is largely irrelevant with regard to the student's success or failure. Competence in one of the two official languages is usually a determining factor of the student's success (O'Brien, Reitz and Kuplowska, 1976). However, language competence in a Native dialect is important when the student completes a post secondary degree and attempts to reintegrate into the Native community or wishes to establish formal links with his/her community (Chartrand, 1985; Prattis and Chartrand, 1985). Any Native occupying a leadership position (or aspiring to such a position) on the reserve or, if off the reserve, wishes to solicit the support of the reserve members, must be fluent in that Native language (Heller, 1988).

While the provincial schools have the potential for providing quality education, Indian success in these educational institutions has been disappointing. Similarly, Indian success in band-operated schools has likewise been disappointing. Its lack of resources as a full professional system is perhaps its most basic shortcoming. However, in both cases, specific factors inhibiting Indian participation in educational institutes have not been identified and there do not seem to by any plans to study the situation in order to remedy it even though over $500 million was spent on education facilities in 1985 alone.

The benefit of training a person in any skill or education will be realized only if the skills have a viable future. That is, only if the person gets the skills and then is able to use them will the training costs, time, and indirect costs be worth it. If an education program is producing people with obsolete or limited demand skills, it is not particularly effective, and is of little use to people who are already undereducated.

Many educational programs direct Natives into jobs that are marginal in existence, highly competitive or low in economic return. In short, although considerable monies are spent on education, they prepare the individual for poverty (DIAND, 1980).

Why have Indian-operated schools been so popular if their performance seems little better than the provincial schools? First of all, the placement of band schools on reserves and administered by Indians is congruent with the overall goal of Indians to achieve self-government. A second reason is that the placement of schools on reserves has provided for considerable employment -- both direct and indirect job creation. Finally, because the federal government values education, Indians have learned to use the school system to negotiate other economic advantages for the community.

Indian Post-Secondary Education

We suggest that Natives attending post-secondary educational institutions be enrolled in a program designed to address problems of status disability. The objective is to create a sense of identity and purpose, a feeling of self-confidence and initiative. To the extent that a program is linked to Native institutions as well as to the educational and occupational institutions, it will establish positions of importance to Native leadership (Stinchcombe, 1965). Institutionalized career sequences must extend from schools serving Native communities into post-secondary institutions, providing a predictable path that regularizes Native participation in all levels of education. The emergence of institutionalized career sequences leading from post-secondary educational institutions into positions of management and leadership of Native communities would further enhance the value attached to schooling at all levels. Native students may be expected to become more committed to completing their education and taking advantage of the opportunities their education will provide.

The program we propose may further isolate Natives on campus but the program will also become the vehicle for expressing and achieving their demands for equality and justice within education as well as in the wider society. To the extent that Natives and non-Natives share the same educational career paths, we may expect that the status order in the larger society will tend to encourage non-Natives to take advantage of and perhaps effectively monopolize available educational opportunities, including opportunities for advancement. Members of the dominant culture may be expected to take the initiative in social interaction, and attempt to control the social agenda (whether by conscious design or by oblivious perseverance). In the presence of efficacious and self-confident non-Natives, most Natives may be expected to be passive and intimidated.

An affirmative action program limited to Natives will mobilize Natives into the education system at all levels. However, such a program may ghettoize many if not most Natives, limiting their ability to take advantage of opportunities controlled by the large public and private organizations that represent the interests of the dominant culture. This strategy may be appropriate for a portion of the student's program, but not advisable for the entire educational career sequence.

While the Indian Act specifies that children between 7 and 16 must attend school, it does not provide the basis for providing post-secondary educational services. Historical precedent as well as a wish to increase the proportion of Natives attending school equal to the national proportion provides the impetus. In carrying out this objective, approximately 93 million dollars is spent each year on ensuring that Natives have access to financial assistance and instructional support services.[9] Two programs operated by Indian Affairs encourage participation in post-secondary education. The first is the university and professional program which provides financial support for those who have been accepted in a post-secondary accredited institution, e.g., university. The second program, the University/College Entrance Preparation Program, enables Natives to qualify for entrance to regular university/ college programs.[10] Although the participation rate of Natives in post-secondary educational institutions has increased over the past decade (from one percent to seven percent), it is no where near the national rate of 20 percent. In numbers, fewer than five hundred Indians graduate from any type of post-secondary institutions each year and few of the are universities. All this suggests that universities have not been successful in educating Native students. The current model adopted by colleges/universities to deal with Natives is to establish a Native Studies Program and process Native students through this structure. However, two decades after they have been in operation, the success of these programs is in doubt. It is time that educators acknowledge the shortcomings of these programs and implement more realistic and operable programs.

Native Studies: A New Program

Existing Native Studies programs have fulfilled their mandate and while they should be maintained, they need to be modified and supplanted for a number of reasons. First of all, many students enrolled in the Native Studies program are not Native. How then, does this benefit the Native student? Some have argued that Natives benefit by non-Indians taking the course in that non-Indians will better appreciate Native culture, as well as hold more positive attitudes toward Natives and their culture. While this may be true, no existing body of literature exists to support such a claim. What data do exist suggests that only students who are already "positively" disposed towards Natives and Native culture take the courses (Sparham, 1978).

Secondly, the production of Native scholars in Native Studies has now exceeded the demand. In short, there are more Native experts on the market than it can bear. Native Studies programs have also tried to teach Native culture to Native students in the program. Again, no literature exists which supports this contention. On the contrary, our discussions with directors of such programs suggest that this is not the case. If this is a goal for Native students, there are many more appropriate contexts in which this socialization should take place, e.g., pow-wows, cultural centres.

The above critique of the Native studies programs is meant to point out that they have outlived their usefulness and modifications and innovations now need to be introduced. We now turn to a modest proposal by the authors as to the direction and structure such programs should have. Some of the ideas have already been partially implemented (Matthiasson and Kristjanson, 1981; Clarke and Mackenzie, 1980).

Our goal is to enhance the status of Natives so that they may deal effectively with non-Natives in face to face interaction. Research spanning over a decade suggests that interracial status expectations can be modified to yield greater equality in interracial interaction (Cohen, 1982, 1985). Cohen has called the two techniques that have proved to be effective expectation training and the multiple ability strategy.

Expectation training involves training members of the subordinate status group to be able to both perform and teach a valued task--any generally valued activity will do so long as (a) members of the dominant status group will be most unlikely to know how to perform the task, (b) members of the subordinate status group will be unlikely to fail when teaching others and (c) the assignment of competence to low status members must be realistic and convincing.

The multiple ability strategy involves convincing students that many different abilities will be required for a multiracial group to accomplish some collective task. Like expectation training, the multiple ability strategy achieves interaction equality by both enhancing the status of students with low status and subordinating the status of students with high status.

The multiple ability strategy and expectation training involved working with small balanced mixed race groups in controlled face to face situations. The program we are advocating to remedy status disability experienced by Natives will have to incorporate such techniques for modifying status expectations, preferably at each stage in the educational sequence. The more frequently these techniques are implemented, the less contrived the situations need be. Indeed, the greater the number of valued activities and tasks that Natives master (and teach to non-Natives), the more the program would take on the character of leadership training. We will begin by identifying each of the central actors.

First of all, a Native Students' Counselling Service should be established. The structure of such an organization would consist of a director, several tutors (the number depending upon the number of Indian students), a counsellor, and a contact person with the community at large.

Let us take each in turn:

(1) **Director**: This individual must have minimum academic qualifications, e.g., Ph.D., M.A. The director must have these in order to achieve legitimacy from within the university community since he/she will give direction to the program. The position occupied by this individual would be equivalent to a Dean of a Faculty and would assume the duties and privileges of such a position. This means that he/she would have direct access to all university administration, e.g., president, vice-president (academic). This individual must also have the ability to establish rules and make certain decisions which would be binding on both the student and the university. This, of course, assumes that the university is fully committed to such a venture. Anything less will only lead to failure.

(2) **Tutors**: Tutors must be qualified academics with a multi- disciplinary background. They can not be transient or part-time staff. Training in cross-cultural affairs and an awareness of problems associated with Natives entering post-secondary institutions would also be necessary. Their basic role is to provide academic expertise for the students. These individuals must liaison with specific faculties/departments and have an adequate understanding of the operation of these units. Our assessment of Native students' performance in university is that they are already motivated to achieve the goal of higher education. Their problem lies in the inadequate preparation of basic skills, both academic and social. For example, most Native students require upgrading in basic writing skills and mathematics since a large component of university work is comprised of written and numerical material.

(3) **Counsellor**: The counsellor would only be part-time for Native students. He/she must be someone with inter-cultural experience or training and be able to speak one of the local Native languages.

(4) **Contact Person**: The central role of this individual would be to liaison between the academic centre, the work place and the Native communities. This individual would need to be sufficiently knowledgeable about the work force as well as informed about employment opportunities and federal and provincial programs related to Natives. In addition, this individual would have access to specific individuals in various companies that would be potential employers of students coming out of the university setting.

A beginning program could handle between 15-25 students. Some type of proportional representation with regard to Metis, treaty, and non-treaty categories could be created. Each of the organizations representing the above groups would be approached and asked for nominations for the most promising students. However, this would not preclude "independent" students from entering the program, and the Native Counselling Service Centre would not be completely bound by these recommendations. The procedure of "nomination and recommendation" legitimizes the selection process and, perhaps more importantly, would establish contacts between the student, Indian leaders and the general Native population.

Each student would be informed at the beginning of the year that his/her experience would be demanding and trying and they would, in essence, be representing the Native people of Canada. In effect, they would be given high status by definition before starting university. The status would be legitimate since such pronouncements would come from a senior official, e.g., Vice-President (Academic), President. This would continue for the duration of their academic studies or until they no longer needed special consideration.

The academic curriculum for Native students attending university would be the same as for any other student. The general philosophy behind the proposed program is that Native students would be placed into status enhancing contexts. These contexts or experiences are necessary to break the stigmatized perspective that now cripples Native people. Two procedures would be used:

A. Native students would undertake and experience status-enhancing experiences well beyond that of the average non-Native student. The first type would centre on social contexts. These experiences would be regular and consistent over the duration of the students' tenure at university. These experiences would be set up by the director, monitored by the director and contact person, but carried out by Indian students. Indian students would be placed in positions where they would interact with politicians, businessmen, community leaders, and academics (all of whom could be either Native or non-Native), as well as with other non-indian students. For example, a Native student would be placed in charge of making arrangements for a local politician visiting the university. This would include meeting the individual at the airport and upon his/her arrival at the university, accompanying him/her to the designated building, introducing the individual as well as making other arrangements. Similar arrangements could be made with visiting academics.

B. The second context would focus on skill enhancement. Native students, during the summer prior to actual entry to university, or during their transitional year would be trained in a number of basic academic skills--writing papers, how to prepare a bibliography, as well as skills related to the activities of university administration. Additional skills would be taught by the tutors during the academic year.

The specific strategy to be employed in "skill advancement" would be to have two Native students learn a particular skill at the same time. Then, after learning the skills, they would "teach" two non-Native students that same skill. For example, first-year students are usually unsure how one drops or adds a course. Native students would be taught this procedure, and then teach non-Native students these skills. Let us take another example. Sociology students are generally unable to understand the structure and implication of a 2 x 2 statistical table. With the help and coordination of the Sociology Department, two native students could be taught this skill. They, in turn, would begin to instruct other non-Native students during the academic year. It should be noted that the pairing of the Native students, in both cases, find themselves in a context which enhances their status, skill and produces positive self-esteem.

Conclusion

We have tried to show that Indian students today are stigmatized, isolated, and have few "self-enhancing" experiences. The program we are recommending would recognize that Indians are different from Whites, but it would not be defined as a negative difference. By design, the differences would illustrate a positive structure. Having a Native student introduce the Premier or the Minister of Education when he visits a campus can hardly be viewed as self-denigration. The consistent frequency of these positive experiences will certainly not eradicate the ethnic differences, but it will illustrate the positive differences.

The resultant student will be well prepared for the outside world when he/she leaves university. Social skills will be well in hand and educational skills will also be in evidence. The Indian student must be forced to undergo a number of painful and potentially embarrassing experiences, just as other students. However, the acquisition of the social and academic skills becomes necessary when he enters the "real world." Native people, at this time, do not have the luxury of producing "marginal" graduates. Perhaps in the future they may have time to do this, but not now.

The issue of identity should not, at least need not, be formally considered at all at the institutional level. However, it is clear that we are arguing that the idea of one's ethnic background should be used, but only in implicit and positive manners. That is, institutions need not be committed to any particular cultural hegemony. Institutions of high education should make provisions of choices which would enable individuals to preserve a particular cultural identity. Multi-culturalism is to be perceived as a phenomenon arising from the exercise in a free country of private initiative, not as living out of the constitutional provisions of the state (Sparham, 1978).

FOOTNOTES

[1] Ideology refers to a set of characteristic ideas, such as principles that reflect social needs and aspirations and are justified by what are perceived as widely held values in society.

[2] Textbooks used in the schools, including toady, have always emphasized "Anglo middle-class" values.

[3] Over the years, various ethnic groups have been ranked by politicians and educators in terms of similarity of values and norms to the dominant group.

[4] Because the school system basically distrusts "variant" ethnic cultures (beliefs and values), the school tries to remold previous beliefs and implant "correct" ideas and behaviour.

[5] In some cases, Manitoba, British Columbia, New Brunswick, have master agreements with the Department of Indian Affairs, whereby a standard tuition fee is based on average costs.

[6] Eighty-two percent of the bands administer part of their education program. Forty percent of these bands are responsible for the total operation of the education program.

[7] Some of the language families are represented by only one language while others contain a number of distinct languages. For example, the Algonquian linguistic group has nine separate distinct languages.

[8] Over the past 15 years, Native language programs have produced few fluent speakers.

[9] It is estimated that there are over twenty thousand students (elementary and secondary) living off the reserve and being educated in provincial schools. The federal government does not accept financial responsibility for these students.

[10] One of the major problems Native students have is meeting the requirements of university entrance.

REFERENCES

Burnaby, B. (1982). *Language in Education Among Canadian Native Peoples*. Toronto: The Ontario Institute for Studies in Education.
____. (1984). *Aboriginal Language in Ontario*. Toronto: Minister of Education, Ontario.
Canada, Government of. (1984). *Canada's Native People*. Ottawa: Minister of Supplies and Services.
____. (1986). *1986-87 Estimate: Part III*. Ottawa: Indian and Northern Affairs Canada, Minister of Supplies and Services.
____. (1985). Indians and Natives. A Study Term Report to the Task Force on Program Review. Ottawa: Minister of Supplies and Services.
____. (1980). *Indian Conditions: A Survey*. Ottawa: Department of Indian and Northern Affairs.
Cave, W. and M. Chesler. (1974). *Sociology of Education*. New York: Macmillan Publishing Co.
Chartrand, J.P. (1985). *Inukitut Language Retention among Canadian Inuit*. Ottawa: Center for Research on Ethnic Minorities, Department of Sociology and Anthropology, Carleton University.
Church, R. (1976). *Education in the United States*. New York: The Free Press.
Clarke, S. and M. MacKenzie. (1980). "Indian Teacher Training Programs: An Overview and Evaluation." In W. Cowan (Ed.), *Papers of the Eleventh Algonquian Conference* (pp. 42-54). Ottawa: Carleton University.
Cohen, E. (1985). *Designing Group Work*. New York: Teachers College Press, Columbia University.
____. (1985). "Expectation States and Interracial Interaction in School Settings." *Annual Review of Sociology*, 8, 209-235.
Cohen, E. and S. Roper. (1972). "Modification of Interracial Interaction Disability: An Application of Status Characteristic Theory." *American Sociology Review*, 37, 648-655.
Collins, R. (1979). *The Credential Society: Historical Sociology of Education and Stratification*. New York: Academic Press.
Craig, J. (1981). "The Expansion of Education." *Review of Research in Education*, 9, 151-210.
Cummins, J. (1981). "The Expansion of Education." *Review of Research in Education*, 9, 151-210.
Davey, R.C. (1965). "The Establishment and Growth of Indian School Administration." In J.W. Chalmers, et al, (Eds.), *The Education of Indian Children in Canada*. Toronto: Ryerson Press.

Fiala, R. and A. Lanford. (1987). "Education Ideology and the World Educational Revolution, 1950-1970." *Comparative Educational Review*, 31, 315-332.

Gordon, M. (1964). *Assimilation in American Life*. Fairlawn, N.J.: Oxford University Press.

Hawthorn, H. (1966-67). *A Survey of the Comtemporary Indians of Canada*. Ottawa: Queen's Printer, Vol. 1 and 2.

Hebert, Y. (1984). "The Socio-Political Context of Native Indian language Education in British Columbia." *The Canadian Journal of Native Studies*, IV, 1, 121-137.

Heller, M. (1988). *Codeswitching: Anthropological and Sociolinguistic Perspectives*. New York: Mounton de Gruyter.

Katz, M.B. (1970). The Hamilton Project, Interim Reports, Working Paper #26. Toronto: O.I.S.E.

Lewin, K., A. Little and C. Colcough. (1982). "Adjusting to the 1980's: Taking Stock of Educational Expenditures." In *Financing Educational Development*, Proceedings of an International Seminar Held in Mont Sainte Marie, Canada. Ottawa: International Development Research Centre.

Matthiasson, J. and R. Kristjanson (1981). Native Students and the Special Nature Students Program at the University of Manitoba, *Culture*, 1, 91-95.

Meyer, J. (1987). "Self and Life Course: Institutionalization and its Effects." In G.M. Thomas, J.W. Meyer, F.O. Ramierez and J. Boli (Eds.), *Institutional Structure: Constituting State, Society, and the Individual* (pp. 242-160). Beverly Hills, California: Sage Publications.

Meyer, J., O. Ramirez, R. Rubinson, and J. Boli. (1977). "The World Educational Revolution, 1950-1970." *Sociology of Education*, 50 (October), 340-363.

O'Brian, G. J.G. Reitz, and O. Kuplowska. (1976). *Non-Official languages: A Study in Canadian Multiculturalism*. Ottawa: Supply and Services, Government of Canada.

O'Neill, F. (1965). "Adult Education in Indian Communities." In J.W. Chalmers, et al (Eds.), *The Education of Indian Children in Canada* (pp. 146-162). Toronto: Ryerson Press.

Prattis, J. and J.P. Chartrand. (1985). *System and Process: Inukitut-English Bilingualism*. Ottawa: Center for Research on Ethnic Minorities, Department of Sociology and Anthropology, Carleton University.

Ramirez, F.O. and J. Boli. (1987). "Global Patterns of Educational Institutionalization." In G.M. Thomas, J.W. Meyer, F.O. Ramirez and J. Boli (Eds.), *Institutional Structure: Constituting State, Society, and the Individual* (pp. 150-172). Beverly Hills, California: Sage Publications.

Siggner, A. (1984). "The Socio-demographic Conditions of Registered Indians." *Social Trends*, Winter, 2-9.

Sparham, R.D. (1978). "Further Education Study," N.W.T. Mimeo.

Stinchcombe, A. (1965). "Social Structure and Organizations: The Relations Between Communities and Organizations." In J.G. March (Ed.), *Handbook of Organizations* (pp.185-191). Chicago: Rand McNally and Company.

Synge, J. (1976). "The Sociology of Canadian Education." In G. Ramu and S. Johnson (Eds.), *Introduction to Canadian Society* (pp. 401-438). Toronto: Macmillan of Canada.

Tamminga, H. (1977). "Past and Present School System Response to Asian Immigrants." A paper presented to the Annual American Sociological Association, Chicago, September.

Toike, R. (1978). "Research Evidence for the Effectiveness of Bilingual Education." *NABE Journal*, 3, 13-24.

Vander Zanden, J. (1965). *Sociology: A Systematic Approach*. New York: Ronald Press.

Whyte, K. (1986). "Strategies for Teaching Indian and Metis Students." *Canadian Journal of Native Education*, 13, 3, 1-20.

INDIAN LANGUAGE PROGRAMS IN SASKATCHEWAN: A SURVEY

Catherine Littlejohn and Shirley Fredeen

Introduction

During the fall of 1986 and the winter of 1987, a survey of Indian language programs in Kindergarten to Grade 12 schools in the province of Saskatchewan was undertaken by the Saskatchewan Indian Languages Institute of the Federation of Saskatchewan Indian Nations. The survey was designed to collect information on the existing programs in provincial, band and federal schools. This research comprised one component of a needs assessment study, other components of which included a literature review (indigenous language education in Canada), a sociolinguistic survey of indigenous language use in Saskatchewan, and the development of a proficiency test for Cree. The overall purpose of the needs assessment study was to enable the Institute to recommend a course of action for the teaching of the languages in Saskatchewan schools, and to set goals and establish priorities for at least the next five years. The study was jointly funded by the Languages Institute and the Saskatchewan Department of Education.

The purpose of the Indian language program survey was to provide a data base on the state of Indian language programming in Saskatchewan schools as of the 1986-87 school year. Specifically, data were sought on: school and school location, type of program, the teaching of literacy, languages taught, funding number of students, training and experience of teachers, who developed the program and when, materials used, and other pertinent information.

Method

Instrumentation

An initial literature search identified research designs and instruments that had been used to investigate similar research questions in the United States and Canada. As a result, a semi-structured questionnaire was developed to collect the data. Four draft versions of the questionnaire were reviewed by personnel from the Community Education Branch, Saskatchewan Education, the Minister of Education's Indian and Metis Curriculum Advisory Committee, particularly those involved with Indian languages, and by noted academics in the area of Indian language research such as Dr. Barbara Burnaby (OISE), Dr. Chris Wolfart, and Dr. John Nichols (both of the University of Manitoba). The instrument was piloted prior to its implementation.

The questionnaires were administered between November, 1986 and March, 1987. They were mailed to participating school principals in November, 1986 with a covering letter requesting their return by December 15. The deadline was extended to January 10, 1987. Every school that had not responded by mid-February was telephoned. Additional copies of the questionnaire were provided at that time to schools that reported that they had not received them. Telephone interviews were conducted in mid-March with principals who still had not returned the questionnaires. This was done in an attempt to ensure a complete data file for those schools that had programs.

Scope of the Study

The study was limited in scope to: (1) all provincial schools in northern Saskatchewan and in urban areas, and all provincial schools in rural areas identified as having more than 15% Indian/Metis students; (2) all Band-controlled schools; and (3) all federal schools (that is, those schools administered by Indian and Northern Affairs Canada). Only publicly-funded K-12 schools were included.

Limitations of the Study

First, the study there was hampered by a lack of accurate and current information on the number of Indian and Metis students in provincial schools in Saskatchewan. Second, the manner in which questionnaires were administered combined with the fact that the return rate was not 100%, a number of schools with programs may not be included in the sample. Some of the questionnaires were self-administered by the principals, some were filled out by the principal in collaboration with the Indian language instructor, some were filled out by Band personnel, while others were completed in a phone interview conducted by the researchers. Finally, as the results were examined, it became evident that there were limitations created by the use of a questionnaire. The terminology and definitions used in talking about language programs for first and second language speakers were not familiar to all of the respondents; therefore, the quality of response could have been improved by the use of interviews rather than questionnaires.

Method of Analysis

The data were coded to opscan sheets and subjected to analysis with the SSPS-X statistical program for the Social Sciences. Frequencies and percentages were tabulated for the structured portions of the questionnaire. The open-ended questions were analyzed by the researchers manually to retain the essence of the qualitative comments.

Rate of Return

Of the 478 questionnaires sent out, responses were received for 327. This represents an overall return rate of 65%. However, the return rate for schools with programs is thought to be 100% as the result of tenacious telephone canvassing of those schools which were known to have had programs.

Findings

Programs

Of the schools responding, 61 reported that Indian languages were used in some form in their school programs. Another 26 schools stated that they had Indian language programs but that they no longer had them. Of the schools reporting that they currently had Indian language programs, 17 were within provincial jurisdiction. Band-controlled schools accounted for 29 of schools with programs and the rest, 15, were federal schools.

All Schools Reporting Indian Language Usage

The following is a summary table of all reported Indian language usage in school programs in Saskatchewan, by language in use.

Language	Language	Dialect	Schools	Enrollment
Algonquian	Cree	Y	38	3902
		TH	11	1456
		N	1	75
	Saulteaux		6	428
Athapaskan	Dene		4	384
Siouan		Dakota	2	72
TOTAL			62*	6317**

Table 1   Indian Language Usage in School Programs in Saskatchewan by Language in Use, 1986-1987.

* This number totals one more that reporting because one school had two languages in its program
** This number is a conservative one because two schools with total enrollment of 479 did not record the number of students in Indian language programs.

As can be seen from Table 1, at least 6317 students in the province of Saskatchewan used an Indian language in their school program in 1986-87. Three distinct Indian linguistic families were in use in schools. Four separate languages were taught and although Cree predominated, schools within the province were teaching three different Cree dialects. The following tables depict the linguistic distribution, the number of schools offering programs, and the student enrolment by each school type (jurisdiction).

Provincial Schools

Two hundred fifty-one provincial schools responded to the questionnaire. Indian languages were used in the programs of 17 or 7% of these schools. Table 2 shows the Indian language usage by language and the enrolment in the Indian language portion of the schools' total offerings.

Language Enrollment	Language	Dialect	Schools	
Algonquian	Cree	Y	12	911
		TH	1	76
		N	1	75
	Saulteaux		2	428
Athapaskan	Dene		1	384
TOTAL			**17**	**1182**

Table 2 Indian Language Usage in Provincial School Programs in Saskatchewan, by Language Used, 1986-1987.

This table demonstrates that 1182 of the students using Indian languages in their school programs in 1986-87 were in provincial schools. This number constitutes 19% of all the students in Indian language programming in Saskatchewan in 1986-87. Three languages were taught and three Cree dialects were evident. The majority of the Indian language usage in the provincial system was in small rural schools. Over two fifths (7 out of 17 or) of those schools reporting programs, were in rural areas in the southern part of the province. Another 7 or 41% of the provincial schools with programs, were in the north. Three city schools (18% of provincial schools with programs) reported using Indian languages in their programs. Two of the schools with Indian languages were in separate schools; one was in the public system.

Band Schools

Twenty-nine of the 53 schools providing data reported Indian language usage within the school program. This means that over half (55%) of the Band schools in the sample were using Indian languages. The following table examines Indian language usage by language.

Language Enrollment	Language	Dialect	Schools	
Algonquian	Cree	Y	16	1962
		TH	10	1380
	Saulteaux		1	206*
Athapaskan	Dene		2	246
Siouan		Dakota	1	42
TOTAL			**30**	**3846**

Table 3 Indian Language Usage in Band School Programs in Saskatchewan by Language Used, 1986-1987
* One school had both Cree and Salteaux. It appears twice in this table.

Federal Schools

Of the 23 schools responding, 15 (65%) had Indian languages in use in their school programs. Table 4 shows the enrolment of students in Indian language programming by language.

Language	Language	Dialect	Schools	Enrollment
Algonquian	Cree	Y	10	795*
	Saulteaux		3	132
Athapaskan	Dene		1	98
Siouan		Dakota	1	30
TOTAL			15	1055

Table 4   Indian Language Usage in Federal Schools in Saskatchewan by Language Used, 1986-1987

*   Two schools did not report the number of students in Indian languages. However, the enrollment of these two schools was 479 and most of these students might have been in Indian language programs. Therefore, the total in Table 4 is conservative.

Types of Indian Language Programs in Saskatchewan Schools

Respondents were asked to identify whether their Indian language programs were intended for students who were already speakers of an Indian language (such programs are termed L1 programs) or whether their programs were designed for students who were not speakers of an Indian language (L2 programs). Within these broad types of programs, those surveyed were asked to indicate what subtype of program their students were involved in. The telephone interviews suggested that some of the administrators were unfamiliar with the terminology and definitions used in Indian language programming. Hence, there may be a discrepancy between the reported data and the actual situations in schools. The following table displays the reported data.

Program Type	L1 B	L2 B	L1 F	L2 F	L1 P	L2 P	T
School Subject	24	19	13	9	10	13	88
Teaching Content	4	1	0	0	1	1	7
Transitional	2	0	1	0	2	0	5
Maintenance	4	0	3	0	1	0	8
Immersion	0	0	0	0	0	0	0
Throughout the Curriculum	0	1	0	0	1	0	2
When Required	1	0	0	0	0	0	1
Conversational	0	0	0	0	2	2	4
All Types	35	21	17	9	17	16	115

Table 5   Types of Indian Language programs Reported, 1986-1987

B = Band Program
F = Federal Program
P = Provincial Program

Note: Since schools could identify more than one type of program which could be both L1 and L2, this table does not include all the number of schools reporting programs.

As can be seen from the table, the majority of programs (88 out of 115, or 77%) entailed teaching the Indian language as one of the subjects in the school curriculum. This was the case for programs intended for non-speakers (L2 programs). Indian languages are used as the language of instruction (including teaching content, transitional, maintenance, throughout the curriculum, and when required) in a minority of cases (23 out of 115, or 20%). An Indian language was used as the medium of instruction in three curricular areas: physical education, language arts, and social studies. Transitional programs, intended for those who enter school not speaking enough English to profit from instruction through English, are those in which an Indian language is used as the language of instruction in the early years, with a gradual transition to English later in the child's schooling. Five such programs were identified. Maintenance programs, in which the use of the Indian language as a language of instruction is maintained throughout the K-12 school program, accounted for 8 of the programs reported. No immersion programs in Indian languages exist in Saskatchewan schools. A small number of individual programs using the Indian language "as required" throughout the curriculum, or providing instruction after school hours for speakers and non-speakers of Indian languages were reported. As noted above, a number of schools reported having programs for both speakers and non-speakers of Indian languages. The fact that both types of students are usually placed in the same program has implications for teacher preparation and curriculum development.

Location of Indian Languages in School Programming

Schools varied with respect to the grade levels at which Indian languages were offered. Table 6 shows the grades at which Indian languages were taught in Saskatchewan schools.

Grade	Band	Fed	Prov.	T
Nursery	10	7	1	18
Kindergarten	21	11	5	37
Readiness	1	0	0	1
One	23	10	10	43
Two	24	11	8	43
Three	25	12	10	47
Four	25	11	12	48
Five	24	11	11	46
Six	22	8	12	42
Seven	18	8	6	32
Eight	15	5	6	32
Nine	13	4	2	19
Ten	9	0	1	10
Eleven	6	0	1	7
Twelve	5	0	1	6
Special Education	1	2	0	0
Alternate Programs	0	1	0	1

Table 6 Grades at Which Indian Languages Were Taught by Type of School, 1986-1987

The above table clearly demonstrates that in 1986-87, Indian languages were in Saskatchewan school programs from K-12, including Special Education and Alternate Education programs. It can be seen that the bulk of students served in the 1986-87 school year were in Grades 1-6, with the number of programs dropping off considerably with each successive year.

Literacy Programs
Table 7 shows the number of schools reporting Indian language literacy programs, and the grades at which literacy training was reported to have been introduced in the three types of schools systems.

Type	Yes	K	1	2	3	4	5	6	9
B	23	4	4	3	4	7	0	0	1
F	12	4	3	2	1	1	0	0	1
P	10	2	1	0	1	1	1	1	0
T	45	10	8	5	6	9	1	1	1

Table 7   Literacy Programs in Indian Languages in Saskatchewan Schools, 1986-1987

In the province of Saskatchewan, 45 schools reported teaching literacy in an Indian language in 1986-87. Most started the literacy program in K-3.

Funding

When the respondents were asked to explain the source and characteristics of the funding for the Indian language programming, the schools in Band and federal jurisdiction showed less variation than did provincial schools. The following quotation is typical of the replies from Band schools was the following quotation:

> There are no specific dollars provided for our Cree language program through Indian Affairs. The band allocates funds through a global budget. So many dollars for each student enroled is [sic] allowed. All subject areas are considered and the total is worked out from there.

Federal schools stated that funds came from regular education budgets, Indian Affairs or other unspecified federal government sources or, as in seven cases, from the Band in the form of payment of the instructor as a band employee.

Provincial schools received their money to operate Indian language programs from a number of sources. Four stated that it came from the province. One indicated that materials were paid for out of the school budget. Two were financed as part of tuition agreements between their school divisions and a Band or Indian Affairs. Two others were directly funded by bands. Grants were used from both Indian Affairs and the Province in various combinations. One school reported receiving Cultural Funds from Indian Affairs for the teacher's salary and the start-up of the program. Another school reported using Divisional/EDF (Educational Development Fund)/Community Schools funds. Yet another school paid the teacher's salary and obtained resource materials with an IMED (Indian and Metis Education Development) grant and provided other resource materials with a grant from Indian Affairs.

Teachers

Numbers

The total number of teachers in the 61 schools reporting Indian language usage in their programs was 69. The 29 Band schools had 37 Indian language teachers. Federal schools and Provincial schools, with the exception of one northern provincial school, indicated that they each had one Indian language teacher. An additional 21 teacher associates, regular classroom teachers and part-time teachers were reported to be teaching an Indian language or using an Indian language for instructional purposes. However, specific information on their qualifications and experience was not included. In the following sections specific aspects of the qualifications are described.

Certification

Table 8 shows the certification of teachers of Indian languages in Saskatchewan schools in 1986-87. According to provincial law, all persons teaching in Saskatchewan schools must have valid Saskatchewan teaching certificates. In 1986-87, Professional "A" Certificates required four years of creditable post-secondary Education resulting in a Bachelor of Education or equivalent degree (for more detailed description, see Saskatchewan Teacher's Federation, 1986). Standard "A" Certificates are no longer issued, and have not been granted since 1985. At that time, they were granted to those who had completed a three-year teacher education program. However, Standard "A" Certificates remain valid for those teachers possessing them. Probationary Certificates are issued on a year-by-year basis to teachers who do not possess the qualifications required for regular certificates. They are requested by a Board of Education when a fully-qualified teacher is unavailable. While Band and Federal schools are not bound by provincial law, they have in practice, tended to use provincial standards as part of their hiring and promotion criteria.

Type	Prof A Cert.	StandA	Prob	Cert.	Not Cert.
B (29)	9	4	3	17*	20
F (15)	1	1	0	2	13
p (17)	4	4	5	13	4
T	14	9	8	32	37

Table 8   Indian Language Teacher Certification in Saskatchewan by School Type, 1986-1987

* One teacher had certification but it was not specified what kind of certification it was.

Of the teachers of Indian languages whose credentials were reported, 32 (45%) had valid Saskatchewan teaching certificates. Of these, 14 (44%) had Professional "A" Teaching Certificates, 9 (32%) had Standard "A" Teaching Certificates, and 8 (25%) had Probationary Teaching Certificates. The largest proportion of teachers with certification were in the provincial system (68%). However, the band-controlled schools had the largest number of highly qualified personnel, with over half of their certified teachers having Professional A certification.

Academic Qualifications

Of the Indian language teachers for whom academic qualifications were noted, only 16 or 23% had university degrees of some kind. The following table shows this.

Type	B.Ed. UofR	B.Ed. UofS	B.Ed.	B.A.	T
B	4	4	1	1	10
F	0	1	0	0	1
P	1	4	0	0	5
T	5	9	1	1	16

Table 9   Indian Language Teacher Academic Degrees by School Type, 1986-1987

Uof R = University of Regina
Uof S = University of Saskatchewan

Twenty-three percent of the Indian language teachers were reported to have university degrees. All but one of these degrees (15) were Bachelor of Education degrees. These degrees require four years of post-secondary education. The B.Ed. degrees reported for these teachers were received from the University of Saskatchewan and the University of Regina, with the majority coming from the University of Saskatchewan.

It was reported that 29 other Indian language teachers (42%) had taken university classes, although they did not have complete degrees. Eight had enough classes to be in third and fourth year B.Ed. programs, while the other 21 were at the first and second year levels.

Specialized Training

The majority of the Indian language teachers (70%) had some training in the form of university classes or workshops. However, it is significant that nearly one-third had no specialized training. Table 10 summarizes this training by school type.

Type	N	Ling	Sec. Lang	Ind. Lang	Other	T
B	26	7	9	22	3	52
F	10	5	6	10	2	23
P	12	5	5	8	2	20
T	48	17	20	40	7	95*

Table 10 Language Teachers with Specialized raining by School Type, 1986-1987

* One teacher may have had more than one specialized class or workshop.

From the accompanying table, it can be seen that, among them, the 48 Indian language teachers who had specialized training had completed 95 classes and/or workshops in the areas of linguistics, second language teaching methods, and Indian languages. The classes have been taken from a variety of institutions: the University of Saskatchewan, the University of Regina (Saskatchewan Indian Federated College), Concordia University and Brandon University. No one university offered a program with all of the specialized courses required.

Teaching Experience and Special Skills

Table 11 gives the teaching experience of the Indian language teachers in Saskatchewan schools by type of school.

Years of Teaching Experience

	1	2	3	4	5	6	7	8	9+	T
B	5	6	7	2	4	-	1	2	6	33
F	2	2	-	2	2	-	1	1	4	14
P	4	1	1	2	1	-	-	1	4	14
T	11	9	8	6	7	-	2	4	14	61

Table 11   Years of Teaching Experience of Indian Language Teachers in Saskatchewan Schools by Type of School, 1986-1987

Of the 61 teachers for whom data were available, 34 (56%) had four or fewer years of teaching experience, while one third had seven or more years of experience.

Special skills, such as Indian language fluency, educational communications, counselling, and home management, were reported for one third of the teachers.

According to principals without Indian language programs, the greatest obstacle to them having programs in their schools was the lack of trained teachers. Thirty-seven (37%) percent of them gave this reason. A concern for 27% of principals without programs was the lack of available materials. Further, almost one quarter of these principals identified the lack of provincially approved courses as a factor that prevented them from having Indian language courses in their schools. The lack of time was seen as a problem by 22% of the 266 principals in the sample who did not have programs.

In addition to the above issues, the principals themselves added 170 comments concerning what prevented them from having Indian language programs in their schools. The following statements fairly well summarize the issues raised.

· The _____ School Division is presently suffering some financial problems and has made cutbacks in this area.
· The school has applied to Heritage Languages for funding and was turned down. We were also told that EDF would not fund salaries so this course was dead.
· We are now negotiating with _____ School Division to increase our staff so that we can hire a Cree instructor).

- We already have trained teachers and time would be no problem.
- Funding is needed--more dollars for materials, to hire an instructor.
- Funding--it would be an addition to our existing programs.
- Funding (3 different schools)

Staffing was another issue mentioned in a variety of ways by the principals. it was often tied to the funding problem, for money was seen as needed to permit an increase in the teaching staff. The following direct quotations express some of the concerns about staffing.

- I cannot teach the Assiniboine language.
- To have an elder come in to teach this would be unfair to that person because they would only be able to teach for short period each time they came. If the school had more grades it would be more feasible, but my children's attention span is somewhat short and it would be a lot of travelling for someone for just a short time each day.
- There is no one on staff who has any background in any language programs for Indians. It would be very difficult (impossible) for a teacher to obtain enough knowledge to teach people who have been speaking a language since they started to talk.
- This is a one-roomed school, hence, there is only one teacher. If an Indian language were to be taught it should necessitate bringing a specialized teacher.
- We do not have staff capable of teaching an Indian language program and the school board is unable to provide an itinerant teacher.

Principals reiterated the fact that a certain number of students are required to justify the implementation of a particular class. In many of their schools, according to this criterion, an Indian language program is not warranted at this time.

- We do not have enough Native students to warrant such a program.
- We were intending to have Assiniboine taught in our school several years ago, but at that time we were not able to get a teacher. However, now with our drop in

enrolments it is becoming a matter of time. Classes are getting smaller and it would be much more difficult to timetable.
· When the program was discontinued the intent was to integrate it into a cultural enrichment program. The program was not implemented however, and now we re experiencing severe budget problems as a result of a drastic drop in enrolment.

Principals expressed the need for more administrative support for Indian language programming.

· When applying for funding for an instructor the proposal goes and is determined by the province-- E.D.F. Someone shod see the need for Indian languages, the people that make the decisions in the department.
· Funding, Department of Education and local board support.
· Department heads need to push harder.
· Commitment from the band authority--it has planned to begin implementation of a Cree language/culture program within the next few years.

If Your School Already Has an Indian Language Program, Do You Have Any Comments on How Your Program Could be Improved?

The following table demonstrates, by school type, the areas for improvement identified by principals with programs.

	TT	M	PR	FD	IN	O
B	9	19	13	6	8	15
F	7	4	14	-	4	6
P	2	2	-	2	1	8
T	18	25	17	8	13	29

Table 12   Areas for Improvement in Indian Language Programs Identified by Principals with Indian Language Usage in Their School Programs, 1986-1987.

TT = Teacher Training   FD = More Funding
M = Materials   IN = More Inservice
PR = Provincial Courses   O = Other

Materials

Materials were the greatest single concern of principals with programs who responded to this question. Band school principals expressed this concern to a greater extent than did other principals, with 66% of all Band principals with programs commenting on it. Some specific statements follow.

- I feel that there is a definite need for more core material. The curriculum for Dene instruction needs to be greatly expanded. there need to be more reference materials and more audio-visual materials. More Dene legends would also help.
- The Indian language instructor prepares a lot of her teaching materials. budget-wise, she finds it difficult to obtain more materials and resources. It makes it difficult when students are not from "Cree" backgrounds but speak their Native languages.
- More materials: more practical, less linguistic.
- There is very little in the way of teaching support materials for Indian language programs. The production and development of Indian language programs could certainly be helpful to Native language instruction.

Provincial Curriculum

Aligned with the issue of materials was the expressed need for a provincial curriculum. This was linked to a perception that standardization is required as well as legitimation. Such courses were seen as providing guides and support materials. Some examples of the specific statements follow.

- Approved by province, K-12.
- A great deal more effort needs to be committed to the development of a Dene language program in both Roman Orthography and syllabics. There is a need for a full curriculum together with associated teacher resources.
- Provincial Curriculum.
- Curriculum Guides required; more materials, books, tapes.
- Standardized curriculum; central agency, materials.
- Native Studies at High School is needed as a complement.

Teacher Training

Teacher preservice and inservice training were important to many of the principals with programs. Thirty percent of the total number of principals with programs raised the issue of teacher training. Twenty-one percent expressed the need for more inservice for their teacher during the school year. Comments on both of these issues are presented here.

- I feel our program is excellent. Having seen a number of Indian language teachers I feel the key is a good teacher. A good teacher must know the material, love the kids and be very demanding of quality work.
- Instructors should have a better understanding of how to teach this program. They need more direction. More classes would be required before they can teach.
- SILTEP should be offered in each district.
- To have trained instructors.
- Training--courses for instructors.
- The teacher should be fluent and teacher-trained.
- Our Cree language instructor has expressed an interest in taking credit classes in Cree language. She would like to have these offered in Prince Albert.
- Certified trained instructors need a training program.
- Availability of certified teachers trained specifically in Cree language teaching.
- There is also a need for a concerted effort to develop a local teacher training program for Indian language teachers in the north--family commitments preclude staff attendance at places such as La Ronge or Prince Albert--such programs must be delivered in Stony Rapids, Black Lake, or Fond du Lac.

Inservice

- More workshops for language teachers.
- (Indian language teachers should) get together more often.
- I also believe that workshops in teaching methods would be valuable.

- There could be orientation workshops for all instructors, particularly new instructors.
- More help in developing curricula for Cree language and cultural programs. Workshops in making the transition from oral Cree to written Cree without having to rely on writing meaningless things just to be busy.

Funding

Many of the principals showed how everything else is tied to the availability of financial resources.

- The potential is here, long range plans are in place; monies however have been a major drawback. Monies must be made available on the local level for instructional materials development, consultation fees, research and training. At this time, these needs have been placed in second priority because of severe cutbacks in funding for our core programs. I am trained curriculum developer with extensive training in bilingual instruction and knowledge of Dakota linguistics. Due to our financial situation, I have had to assume other duties (administrative and resource instruction) in order to assure that minimal services are provided at our school. With the limited time I do have available, I have developed some things but we do not have the money to have them published.
- Our Cree language instructor is attempting to meet the needs of 340 students. We need either a full-time aide or another full-time Cree language instructor. unfortunately, this translates into dollars that are unavailable at this point in time.
- At the present, the five Cree language teachers teach only in their own classrooms because (mainly) of staff reductions announced last spring due to financial constraints. As soon as finances allow (next year I hope) there should be a certified teacher given the responsibility--and the time--for a regular Cree language program--eventually from Kindergarten through Grade 12. But first we'll have to build a solid program at the Division I and II levels, utilizing the Cree-speaking teachers we have, but with overall co-ordination by one teacher who is given the time to do a good job.

Other Suggestions

A large number of principals offered other suggestions for improving their programs. Increasing the cultural content and involvement of local resource people led the lit of proposals.

- Possible to spend more time on the history of the Indian people to relate it to the language. There is a need to instill as much pride as possible in Indian children.
- Our Dene language program is going quite well now due to the enthusiasm of our instructor, _____. One way in which our program could develop would be in the area of history and culture. It would be beneficial to have a greater source of information concerning the language and dialect roots of the local people as well as greater understanding of the culture which is so much a part of the language.
- It would help a lot to have an Elder come into the classroom at least once a week to influence the students in the values of our heritage and culture.
- In order to facilitate Indian language programs in a more effective way, I feel that local resources should be utilized to the maximum: ie. elders, local history, legends, story-telling etc. Obviously, this would require budget money. This should be stressed at the Indian Affairs level.

The following are individual comments made by principals, which give a further perspective on Indian language programs in Saskatchewan schools.

- I wish that we could extend our Cree program right up to Grade 12 but due to non-availability of funds, trained teachers and lack of material we are compelled to keep the program only up to Grade 4. Once the younger generation loses the language, there is a grave possibility of losing identity.
- There should be more suggestions or options in the testing procedure. The method used at the present time is oral testing. It is effective but very time consuming. For 90 Students it takes 2 weeks to test them all.

Needs Expressed

Principals were asked whether there had been a need expressed for an Indian language program. Forty-three principals stated that a need had been expressed. Of this number, 35 (81%) were from provincial schools. Over one third (34%) of the provincial schools which reported that a need for Indian language programming had surfaced were in urban areas. Twenty-three percent or eight schools were in the north. An equal number were in other rural schools. Support for Indian language programming was reported to have com from parents, local boards of trustees, teachers, students, school system personnel, local Band Chiefs, Band councils and Band Education committees.

The principals were very generous in offering many comments. When asked for final additional information, many elaborated on the need for programs or reasons why programs were not necessary. Most of their views have been discussed in previous sections. However, some ideas which appeared in this section bear repeating. These include:

- Both funding and program policies have to be established.
- Introduce Indian languages to NORTEP. Recommend to universities.
- (Our) Division should address it as a Division. It should be mandatory to teach the language--culture aspect and language.
- We would be willing to pilot a language program.
- I believe that there should be support to offer an Indian language as a high school credit.
- Should some students be taking Cree instead of French?
- There could be a program offering, at least within an area encompassing several schools in our area.
- My experience in Native language instruction leads me to believe that Native language at the Division I level should be in the form of immersion or not at all.
- I personally do not believe that there is any concerted opposition to Indian language programs. They simply have not been offered, and the public has accepted this situation to date.
- I believe that interest should be stimulated and the opportunity for a program created. Cree would be a logical choice and perhaps should be integrated with a strong cultural/historical component--but it should definitely be available to non-Native students too.

- A needs assessment would have to be carried out. If it was found to be a priority for students and their parents, then, yes.

Summary, Conclusions, and Recommendations

Summary

This study reported on Indian language usage in Saskatchewan school programs by school principals across the province. The data were collected through semi-structured questionnaires administered between October 1986 and March 1987. A total of 327 questionnaires were returned. It was found that 61 schools had Indian language usage in their school programs. Of these, 17 were provincial schools. Four of these were in the north. There were 29 Indian language programs in Band-controlled schools and 15 in federal schools.

In Saskatchewan, there were at least 6317 students studying one of the Indian languages in schools during the 1986-87 school year. Cree (Y dialect) was being learned by 3902; Cree (TH dialect), by 1456; Cree (N dialect), by 75; Saulteaux, by 428; Dene, by 384; and Dakota, by 72. The majority of these students were being taught the Indian language as a school subject with a specific time in the timetable. Slightly more programs were reported for children who were already speakers of an Indian language than for non-speakers. Although Indian languages were being taught in every grade from Nursery to Grade 12, including Special Education, most of the students served were in Grades 1-6. Literacy in an Indian language was being taught in 45 of the 61 schools that had programs.

Funding to support Indian Language programs in schools was reported to be within the regular eduction budget in most Band and federal schools. However, provincial schools attempting to offer Indian languages reported that it was necessary to look for funding from a variety of sources, much of it on a short-term grant basis. Many of the schools indicated that cutbacks in funding affected the Indian language programs before the "core subjects". Five of the provincial schools that discontinued programs cited a lack of funding as the reason for the programs' demise.

Information was provided for 69 Indian language teachers from the 61 schools offering programs. An additional 20 individuals--aides, regular classroom teachers, and unspecified others--were reported to have been teaching Indian languages, but no data were included for them. The teaching staff for whom information was provided were generally uncertified (37 out of 69), but had some university classes (44 out of 69) and/or workshops (48 out of 69) in specialized areas related to Indian language teaching such as linguistics, second language teaching methods, and Indian languages. These courses were selected from a variety of universities to suit the needs of individual teachers. About one-third of the Indian language teachers had taught for seven or more years while another 30% had only one or two years' experience. Therefore, the majority of these teachers had over three years' experience.

With a few exceptions, Indian language teachers were hired on a full-time basis. However, the majority of them spent less than 70% of their time teaching the Indian language but had very little in-school planning and preparation time: one to three hours per week for 70% of the teachers. The Indian language teachers reported that they had other duties in the school, in addition to language teaching. Some Indian language teachers reported that they had other duties in the school, in addition to language teaching. Some Indian language teachers were regular classroom teachers. In other cases their duties included taking on entirely different roles such as a teacher of a different subject area, teacher aide, resource room teacher, or counsellor.

Indian language teachers reported that they had the opportunity to attend inservice activities once or twice a year. Salary scales of Indian language teachers were not always consistent with the school system that the teacher worked for the increments did not necessarily accrue from experience and education.

The materials which the Indian language teachers were using were limited in scope and quantity. Language teachers through necessity were creating their own materials, developing their own curricula, and devising their own programs. They made extensive use of the materials that they were aware of, even if they were not designed for the Indian language that they were teaching. They adapted from other Indian language materials. They translated from English language materials and they adjusted materials for teaching English as a second language. They integrated cultural materials into their courses with books and films. Despite the fact that Indian language teachers were material developers by necessity, less than half of the schools reported any available funds for materials development. What money there was, was generally provided by sources other than the provincial government or the community. Generally it was part of a special grant from Indian Affairs or a Band.

Indian language teachers seemed to have access to all of the audiovisual equipment a regular classroom teacher would need. However, they were not generally equipped with language specific aids such as language labs, listening stations and computers. Less than half of the Indian language teachers had their own classroom. This meant that over half of the Indian language teachers had nowhere to call home in the school, nowhere that the students could retreat to when they wanted to speak the Indian language to the teacher alone. There was nowhere that the teacher could claim to have students work, to leave materials displayed, to clutter with the business of materials development. There was nowhere for these "homeless" teachers to bring the Indian parents to show them where the Indian language happened. The evidence from the study showed that Elders and resource people were not often part of the school program. However, many of the principals indicated that they thought involving resource people was a good idea. There needs to be more information on the ways resource people, and Elders in particular, are brought into the existing programs and what prevents the more extensive use of their expertise.

The study showed a strong support for the idea of teaching Indian languages among the principals in the sample. One hundred and twenty-five thought that it was a good idea for their school. Sixty-five of these principals were from schools without programs: 54 from provincial schools, six from Band schools, and five from federal schools. These principal's support was buttressed by the evidence that there had been a need for Indian language programs expressed directly to 43 principals. Major obstacles to the implementation of such programs were identified as: funding; a lack of trained teachers; a lack of materials for certain age/grade level and linguistic groups; a lack of provincial approval, policy, guidelines and standardized curriculum; a lack of administrative commitment and support at the local level, division level, regional level, provincial level, federal level (Indian Affairs), district level (Indian Affairs and Indian District Chiefs Councils) and Band level. Although not all of these levels were castigated to the same extent, each was specifically singled out by at least one of the principals.

The responses of the principals were for the most part very thoughtful. They provided very detailed comments were they felt elaboration of their concerns was necessary. Even when they did not believe that it was appropriate for them to have an Indian language program in their school, they made suggestions about language program in their school, they made suggestions about ways to provide the service to those students in their schools who might want it. Many of their suggestions have been incorporated into the recommendations which follow.

Conclusions and Recommendations

The results of the study point to the need for a public discussion of the issues around Indian languages. There is a high degree of interest in the Indian languages but the debate with regard to their place in the school program has been waged with regard to their place in the school program has been waged on a local basis which has resulted in a general lack of information about: the research base for arguments of pedagogy as well as culture; materials; other programs (even in neighbouring schools); the steps involved in implementing a program; and the realities of deciding what program type is appropriate for the clientele. the study has demonstrated the need for a comprehensive system to support and encourage Indian language usage in Saskatchewan schools.

Recommendations Regarding a Support System for Indian Language Usage in Saskatchewan Schools

1. The system should involve a mechanism for collaboration among the Department of Education, the Federal Government, the Universities, Indian and Metis Governments, and local representatives in specified areas.
2. The support system should include a program policy statement, a philosophical framework and a rationale for types of programs and their appropriate usage.
3. It should include a rationalization of funding for programs, teacher training, transportation for students, inservice teacher salaries and increments, curriculum development and materials production.
4. Mechanisms for informing administrators about programs, resources, and policy should be established.
5. A teacher training program should be approved at both the Saskatchewan Indian Federated College (University of Regina) and the University of Saskatchewan to specifically train teachers of Indian languages and to accommodate those Indian language teachers who have courses already.
6. Inservice programs should be arranged specifically to meet the needs of the current Indian language teachers. Workshops and newsletters should be instituted as a way to bring ideas and experience together in order to support the teachers in the field.
7. Support should be provided in the area of curriculum development and materials production through workshops consultative services, implementation packages, and central distribution of key materials.

Recommendations Regarding Implementation
1. Guidelines should be established as to what action is taken when parents request programs.
2. Guidelines should describe the various program alternatives in terms of their characteristics, resource requirements, goals and expected outcomes.
3. Guidelines should include the principles that govern what number of students constitutes a sufficient number for a program n a school. They should also address the issue of what constitutes a suitable group at one level in second language programs.
4. Guidelines should be established that provide for transitional, maintenance or English as a second language programming for students with an Indian language as their first language.
5. Guidelines should make provisions for an assessment of the language teaching within schools taking into account the delivery of the communication component of he Common Essential Learning as well as the Required Areas of Study and the method of delivery, time and all aspects that affect the child's language learning.
6. Guidelines should take into consideration situations where for enrichment and pedagogical reasons, Indian languages are integrated into the total curriculum.
7. Guidelines should suggest programs, methods and techniques which enable the school to meet the needs of heterogeneous classes (speakers and non-speakers of the Indian language).
8. Pilot projects should be set up for various experimental programs: immersion; a magnet school (where students are bussed to a school which provides special language programming); a laboratory school incorporating all aspects that should support a successful program, according to the research.
9. Existing bilingual and core programs should be studied and research reports should be made available to practitioners and other researchers.

Recommendations Regarding the Teaching Conditions of Indian Language Teachers
1. Guidelines should be set establishing a uniform salary grid for Indian language teachers in Saskatchewan, a grid which provides incentives for education, experience, and specialised training.
2. Guidelines should be put in place to support the equipping of schools with the appropriate teaching aids for Indian languages such language labs, listening stations, and computers, especially for language groups who could link up

with others in their language group who live in other communities, other provinces, or in the United States. Mechanisms for providing Indian language teachers with their own classrooms should be created.

References

Saskatchewan Indian Languages Institute. (1987).
 Indian Language Program Survey Report: Saskatchewan K-12 Programs. Saskatoon: Federation of Saskatchewan Indian Nations.
Saskatchewan Teachers' Federation. (1986).
 Teacher Certification and Classification in Saskatchewan. Saskatoon: STF.

LEARNING PROCESSES AND TEACHING ROLES IN NATIVE EDUCATION: CULTURAL BASE AND CULTURAL BROKERAGE

Arlene Stairs
Queen's University

Introduction

Reflecting the historical foundations of all formal schooling, language has been our primary focus in developing native and minority education in Canada (Burnaby 1982, Cummins 1983). Early initiatives in native education focused on teaching the dominant language (usually English) to native children. As the philosophy and policy of multiculturalism took hold over the last decade, our focus expanded to bringing native languages into the formal school setting. Native languages were first taught as cultural inclusion programs--limited components appended to the mainstream curriculum--and remain as distinct native language courses in many parts of the country. These programs gradually moved beyond language to include elements of native cultural content, and in certain regions native language spread into lower levels of the standard primary curriculum. With rare exceptions, however, the learning-teaching processes in the education of native children have been unaffected by this inclusion of native language and content. In Canada, as in the American native schools studied by Susan Philips (1983: 133):

> Surprising little attention has been given to the teaching methods used in teaching ethnic minority children in this country, particularly when the notion of culturally relevant curriculum materials has been around as

long as it has. It is as if we have been able to recognize that there are cultural differences in what people learn, but not in how they learn [italics added].

My first purpose in this article is to explore what we are beginning to discover (or rediscover) about the "how" of native learning--about traditional native processes of education. I seek to show that the linguistic and curricular content of native education (see Leavitt in this volume) can be adequately pursued only when embedded in traditional cultural values concerning ways of using language, of interacting, and of knowing. Secondly I examine how brokerage between native (traditional) and school (formal) learning processes is being concentrated in the new cultural role of "native educator". I try to face and objectivize the strong subjective feelings and conflicts arising when process and role are added to language and content issues in native education. In conclusion, I try to map out a path, should we choose to follow it, from language and cultural inclusion to broad cultural base in native Canadian education.

Native Learning-Teaching Processes

North Baffin Inuit recognize radically different concepts of education (Wenzel in press). I will borrow the Inuit concept labels to help my discussion of native learning and teaching processes, acknowledging that our grasp of the full implications of these two different approaches to knowledge is far from complete.

Isumaqsayuq is the way of passing along knowledge through observation and imitation embedded in daily family and community activities, with integration into the immediate shared social structure as the principal goal. The focus is on values and identity, developed through the learner's relationship to other persons and to the environment. In contrast, ilisayuq is teaching which involves a high level of abstract verbal mediation in a setting removed from daily life, with the skill base for a future specialized occupation as the principal goal. While conventional formal schooling reflects many ilisayuq features, certainly some features of isumaqsayuq are paralleled in such current non-native educational movements as experiential education and whole-language approaches. It is suggested here, however, that we are just beginning to comprehend native learning models in terms of their rich, historical integrations of ecological, social, and cognitive cultural systems (Stairs 1988b, and see references in Conclusion below).

Ecological Culture

Isumaqsayuq is perhaps most obviously distinguished from formal schooling or ilisayuq by its adaptive fit into native ecology and economy, that is, into the traditional material culture. Mistakes are more critical in real settings than in protected learning situations, thus extended observation before first attempts is more functional in traditional life than is the trial-and-error learning encouraged in modern formal education. Because the use of acquired skills in very particular community tasks is the goal of traditional learning, education in real-world settings, "in context", makes sense. Inuit and other native children are often taught through a process of "backwards chaining" in which final steps of essential adult tasks are progressively left undone for children to complete, thus giving them an immediate and important role in community work. A young girl may first complete the final trim on her father's new pair of kamiks (skin boots), then the next year sew together several of the cut pieces as well as trimming. She would do the initial skin preparation and cutting only when older, not as isolated early steps in the learning process.

Native learners typically develop concepts and skills by repeating tasks in many different situations, such as hunting under varying conditions of weather and animal movement, and with various types of equipment. They do not traditionally make explicit verbal formulations of basic ideas or rules for success, but rather recount what they have experienced and listen to stories which present concepts and principles implicitly. Formulation of the big ideas is left to the mind of individual participants or listeners according to their own experience levels and perspectives. Clues for appropriate uses of language in formal native education might be found in this contextualized verbal aspect of isumaqsayuq (Scollon and Scollon 1981).

Teachers unfamiliar with the type of contextualized education exemplified by isumaqsayuq often worry that students do not "know" a particular topic or concept when they cannot verbalize the knowledge; they assume that verbal abstraction is a necessary mediating step in high level understanding. Teachers may also conclude that native students are not involved in their learning when they reject early attempts at a new skill, or that they are lost and unable to learn a skill when they fail at preliminary isolated steps. In fact, however, in a situation such as an introductory computer programming class, a non-participating native student may be watching the process until she or he feels ready for a proficient first try or until a real-world practical application, such as preparing graphics for a community newspaper, becomes apparent and contextualizes the skill being learned.

Many steps of school learning, as in the mathematics requirements for technical and scientific careers, are even more widely removed than this computing example (often by years) from target skills as practised by competent adults. Native teachers and parents, for their part, sometimes worry that a great deal of such decontextualized ilisayuq education may be damaging to children in pushing them beyond relevant experience and outside ecological harmony. Traditionally, children's learning is monitored by their direct testing of social and environmental reactions. New skills, such as adjusting a ski-doo starter or organizing a toss game, either work in the real world or they do not; there is no need for mediation by a specialized teaching authority who passes or fails the new learning. The praise and punishment so central to the "push" of ilisayuq are in isumaqsayuq either the positive inclusion of the child in community activity or the negative non-responses--and sometimes teasing--of the group (Briggs 1979). In its potential for overloading students with content disconnected from lived experience, ilisayuq can conflict with the native view of children as complete beings who are in charge of their own development and not to be directly formed by adult manipulation.

Social Culture
It must already be clear that isumaqsayuq not only integrates teaching and learning into traditional material culture but also transmits Inuit social culture. Isumaqsayuq is characterized by the ultimate value placed on group cohesion. Awareness of interpersonal relationships and one's role in the social network is what constitutes maturity; this social competence has priority over individual excellence and productivity. In small communities, where interdependence is necessary for survival and where there is little choice in companions or co-workers, the goal of education is group rather than personal self-sufficiency. Cohesion is supported through extensive interactions among learners and between learners and teachers. Roles of learners and teachers continually shift, and the learning of skills and knowledge from a wide range of teachers is embedded in and subordinate to the learning of skills and knowledge from a wide range of teachers is embedded in and subordinate to the learning of multiple kinship and social roles. Knowledge is a shared resource acquired cooperatively. This "circle of learning" (Harrison 1982) is demonstrated as older siblings teach newly acquired skills to younger ones, and is evident even in formal higher education when, for instance, adults returning from courses or conferences immediately present new information to their communities.

Perhaps paradoxically on the surface, native social cohesion is seen to rest on individualism. The community respects individual differences within the bounds of cultural norms, and takes advantage of the various talents among its members--a leader's political skill, a hunter's knowledge of animals, a storyteller's ways with words, a businessman's financial ability. Young learners, too, are accepted as individuals and are not expected to progress all in the same direction at the same time nor to meet set standards of achievement. They are expected to attend to adult activities around them according to their own motivations, or to approach teachers and elders themselves, before direct instruction is given. The cultural resilience of learner-initiated education and the focus on social cohesion is revealed in recent reversals of expected teaching and learning roles. An Inuk elder, speaking at a circumpolar symposium on the future of native education, and a Shuswap leader, in a video documenting community recovery from alcoholism and economic failure (both in 1985), advised others not to reject but to respect, approach, and learn from their formally-educated children.

The social structure of isumaqsayuq is easily and often misunderstood in ilisayuq classrooms. In formal schools, where maturity is equated with the achievement of autonomy and individual success, observation and cooperation may be interpreted as inattention or even "cheating". Personal relationships between teachers and learners are discouraged as distracting students from achievement and generating teacher favouritism. Teachers keep social distance in the classroom in order to evaluate and rank students by periodically assessing independent products. This kind of final evaluation differences sharply from evaluation in traditional learning where mastery is "kept open" (Annahatak 1985) and refined through continual social and environmental feedback.

The possibility of such "open" learning in school settings was demonstrated in an upper primary class making beginning reading booklets for younger children. Students worked in groups with no clear leaders, variously contributing art work, writing, or technical skills according to their abilities and interests, helping and correcting each other and responding to the reactions of their young reader clientele. The teacher was essentially a team member and a resource in this learning activity, providing students with requested information and skills (such as word spellings or a binding technique) rather than judging and grading their individual contributions. Evaluation of the booklets was largely qualitative and was on a group rather than individual basis. The work was highly contextualized, both materially and socially, and much of the evaluative feedback to the students came continually and directly from their work environment. Native educators making such attempts to introduce isumaqsayuq social structure into schools may find that the competition inherent in the usual individual isolation of formal teaching and evaluation, particularly the recognition of star learners or the identification of failures, is inimical to their primary purpose--successful group cohesion in learning.

In general, teachers from either a formal or a traditional background observe in students of the "other school" what they see as that system's shortcomings. Native teachers find that many non-native children are unaware of the network of social roles, the orienting social context, surrounding the skills and information they are acquiring. They do not internalize what they learn and "do not know what they know" until confirmed by a teacher. One can observe, for example, a junior high school boy learning metal working as an industrial arts subject, with his productions judged only by a professional teacher in a classroom setting--a skill for which he has neither the need, social structure, nor equipment to apply for himself or others at home. In contrast, one can observe a native child learning to hunt ptarmigan with his older brothers, using tools he is also learning to construct--skills which will contribute food to and help define his social role in his family and his community.

Teachers in formal settings find equally disturbing shortcomings in traditional native education. They see self-initiated learning as incompatible with the modern world--too accepting of deviance and learning weaknesses, too inefficient for use with large numbers of students, too random and too parochial in face of the vast range and complexity of contemporary knowledge. From both formal and traditional educational perspectives, a key to dealing with the perceived shortcomings and incompatibilities of the other perspective may be recognition of the social nature of these differences. Interesting and unanswered questions concern the extent to which students can learn non-native information and concepts through isumaqsayuq interactive processes, and the extent to which relatively decontextualized learning processes characteristic of ilisayuq can be used to acquire native knowledge and skills.

Cognitive Culture

At the cognitive level, isumaqsayuq and ilisayuq are comprehensive systems which guide the life and learning of individuals within their cultural contexts. As described by a native educator (Annahatak 1985), cognitive culture underlies a people's outward material and social expressions of their culture and integrates the affective ("what they feel... and value") and perceptual ("what their minds make them see") with the intellectual ("the way they imagine and design...their way of thinking and language [sic]"). A people's cognitive model of the world is evident in the ways they organize knowledge (see examples in Leavitt this volume). In studying native learning and teaching processes, culturally different ways of knowing are not to be compared according to some assumed acultural criterion of pedagogical effectiveness. Rather these differences in cognitive culture are to be seen as peoples' collectively-preferred ways of thinking about the world, each way offerings insights not available to others.

Isumaqsayuq validates knowledge on the basis of life experience and community consensus. This knowledge is conveyed holistically and thematically. From the panoply of her own and her people's relationships with dogs, for example, Mitiarjuk Nappaaluk, an Inuk elder, has provided material for Qimminuulignajut ilumiutartanngit [The dog book] (c. 1985) which synthesizes knowledge categorized by non-natives as biology; skills and economics of hunting, transportation, food, and clothing; art forms; animal behaviour and training; history; man/animal/environment cosmology; myths and tales, feats, disasters, and social roles of dogs. Native teachers typically provide meaning in this way, by relating a theme to a number of real-life experiences and feelings, recognizing that children do not learn "one thing at a time" (Wolcott 1982).

Ilisayuq validates knowledge on the basis of objective proof and expert opinion. It conveys knowledge in abstract universal categories (for instance, insects, fish, mammals, or science, philosophy, art) rather than situational specifics, and it organizes these categories into hierarchies rather than treating each in its own right. Learners are isolated from one another and from their teachers, and generally removed from the social context of their learning. They find themselves required to learn in unfamiliar ways, maybe most significantly having to make distinctions between thinking and feeling, lest one interfere with the other. These deep contrasts of formal thinking with traditional cognitive culture have largely unexplored implications for all aspects of native education, from teaching practices to research. Some contemporary native educators are demonstrating possible cognitive meetings between formal and traditional learning processes. The younger, formally educated Inuk who prepared The dog book for classroom use cut Mitiarjuk Nappaaluk's material into strips which were then arranged by educational topic. These topics, however, such as "What young dogs do" and "How dogs are pregnant", were still more contextual than textual, and the richness of social, perceptual, and affective elements was preserved.

Cultural Conflict or Cultural Brokerage?

At a recent major education conference in the Northwest Territories--Canada's region of highest proportion native population--participants rejected the potential political and personal conflicts of officially discussing the process issues of native education. Planned sessions on culture-based education were cancelled shortly after they began. Also this past year, both native and non-native students in a Concordia

University native education course were uncomfortable with the necessity, as they initially understood it from the viewpoint of formal education, to oppose and choose between isumaqsayuq and ilisayuq. At least some moved towards accepting juxtaposition of the two models of learning and teaching processes without, for the present, attempting to reconcile them. Most responded both to the excitement of expanding their teaching repertoires by using the two approaches, and to the difficulties generated in school settings by the meeting of these two profoundly different systems of human learning. "One-headed" and "two-headed" possibilities in the meeting of isumaqsayuq and ilisayuq were discussed: either the eventual integration of the two models into a new cultural pattern of learning and teaching, or the continuing existence of two distinct models used according to situation and in complement to each other. As I now examine, these possibilities become manifest largely through the roles of educators, particularly of native teachers, as culture brokers in the meeting of isumaqsayuq and ilisayuq.

Native Educator Roles

Five years ago, in her study of learning in a native Alaskan village, Barbara Harrison (1982: 108, 192) observed that "orientation for new (non-native) teachers often consisted of nothing more than instruction in how to do the paperwork." "It was the Yu'pik children," she concluded, "who were left to resolve the conflicting expectations between the way they were expected to learn in informal settings and the way they were expected to learn in school." Certainly in some multicultural settings both native and non-native educators have become more effective in recent years. However it has been curriculum more often than teachers themselves that has changed. Certain changes in non-native teacher roles which are directly implied by recent curriculum developments in native education have occurred--changes such as teaching second language primarily through the conversation, storytelling, and talking-while-doing typical of students' linguistic communities (Leavitt this volume). Here I will examine the changes and the new roles which formal education is demanding of native teachers, and the insights which this native experience can offer all educators.

The culture-based approach to native education recognizes teachers as the immediate agents of contact--and therefore of conflict or reconciliation--between diverse cultural learning models. Teachers bring with them not only their fund of knowledge, but also their culturally-patterned ways of organizing and passing on that knowledge. Even more fundamentally, they bring the value systems of their communities concerning what is important to learn and how it is most appropriate to learn it. Unlike the paper-managers observed by Harrison, teachers in a culture-based program have as their first priority to establish classroom processes of learning and teaching which connect with the patterns of adult-child and child-child relationship expected by their students and the community. It is significant for the validity of this culturally based approach to educator roles that in many native traditions teachers are considered an integral part of the knowledge they possess, and their ways of teaching are as important as the knowledge itself (Cooley and Ballenger 1983: 97-99).

The dual role of teachers, as socio-cultural agents and as technical educators (Piddington 1951), is evident at several levels in culture-based native education programs. The teacher is first of all a culture broker between native and non-native, selecting and transmitting to students her or his personal synthesis of knowledge, values, and human relationships gleaned from cultures in contact. At a practical level, this brokerage involves the dual role of looking to students for clues about the best ways to help them learn within the formal education system, and simultaneously searching the system itself for modifications to allow more appropriate responses to the needs of native students. Most native teachers are also faced with the input task of collecting and structuring bicultural information and methods--from such diverse sources as elders, linguistic specialists, media, politicians, assorted consultants, and their own students--as well as with the output task of conventional teaching. Native teachers must be jacks of all educational trades. Lack of existing programs for many native situations and rapid cultural change make this input-output duality a constant feature of native educators' roles.

Native educators additionally function as brokers within their own communities, seeking to find the best balance between the divergent goals of education for economic advancement and education for cultural maintenance (Bullivant 1984). In doing so, they serve the community as cultural translators between native and non-native life- and learning-styles. In traditional communities, the teacher is often chosen by the population and feels her or his job to be a "calling" comparable to that of a priest. In addition to requiring professional competence, this calling demands that native teachers live in the awareness that they are cultural role models for students and others. They must integrate their professional teaching with the daily informal learning-teaching interactions of the villagers--interactions which consistently place skill and knowledge acquisition within the context of local social values (Briggs 1983). A native professor of languages and education insists that teachers in a native village "must be products of that community in order for the children to learn the value system of the community" (MacLean, in Curwin, 1986: 21).

Clearly the roles of a native and a non-native educator is ostensibly the same position, even in the same school, differ in multiple ways which are rarely recognized in formal job descriptions. Most basically, non-native teachers identify primarily with the formal education system and strive to bring the community into the school, while native teachers identify with their communities and strive to make the school a significant part of the students' community life. Many Inuit teachers in the eastern Arctic keep grounded in their community culture by alternating over the years between professional education and non-professional family roles. While it is a promising creative response to culture contact, such cycling does not solve all the problems of life as both an intimate member of a native community network and a formally-trained teaching professional. Teachers are expected, for example, to deal in the same way with all students and with all colleagues. When the group of students is made up of children in differing kinship and social relationships to the teacher, and when professional colleagues are sometimes family authority figures or proteges, the conflicts between traditional and formal roles can be intense. The quest for isumaqsayuq/ilisayuq brokerage is as critical for native educators as it is for native students.

Both the cultural conflicts and the creative reconciliations in native educators' roles are perhaps best illustrated by current developments in native teacher education (Stairs 1988a). Native educators have been seen to progress through three stages (extended from Beebe, in Modiano 1974-75):

- a "chaotic" stage of mismatch between traditional informal teaching and the formal education structure, as when a community elder, asked into the school to "teach" carving, works quietly in the corner of the room, while a group of teenagers, used to imposed direction in the classroom, drifts into disruptive activity;
- a "cookbook" stage, in which native teachers adopt the formal methods demonstrated to them, even to the point, in a typical instance, of having students number the lines in their written work, thereby religiously following a methodological quirk of a favoured non-native teacher education instructor;

- a "reconstruction" stage, in which native teachers integrate at least some aspects of schooling back into their culturally valued processes of learning, exemplified by an Inuk teacher who takes his class out into their community to help elders with repairs and getting water in exchange for legends and stories, old words no longer in common use, and demonstrations of sled-making and string games.

Until recently, native teachers only rarely reached the reconstruction stage. Where this third stage of teacher development has been reached, it has generally involved exceptional individuals who were able to maintain their cultural grounding despite long periods of training time away from their roles and identity base in the native community. Certain genuinely culture-based approaches to native teacher education are beginning to overcome this professional development barrier, and may be generally easing the cultural conflicts facing contemporary native educators. In particular, a field-based apprenticeship approach responds to the need, expressed urgently by native teachers, to be providing immediate effective teaching to their children rather than leaving their communities for continued professional development. Successful application of the apprenticeship approach builds on the preferred isumaqsayuq learning mode of native educators, including "circle of learning" processes through which more advanced educators continually pass on their experience and training by working with newer teachers. In at least one instance, these knowledge-sharing cycles of instruction have made possible a complete first-language, first-culture teacher education program, to full certification and degree level, carried out entirely in Canada's most isolated communities (Stairs 1988a).

To what extent is it possible, and desirable, for native educators to synthesize traditional and formal teaching? Many native elders fear that traditional skills and approaches to knowledge will be trivialized or perverted by formal educators; that the informal teaching role of the community will be destroyed; and that the overriding educational goal of social cohesion will be abandoned. Despite deep concern over seeing their children drift away from community tasks and into escapism as they progress through school (e.g. Sindell 1987), parents also fear that children taught native ways into school will not acquire mainstream ways and so will not be able to cope in either world. Linguists, mindful of historical examples, worry that native languages will become assimilated through formal teaching or lost in universal bilingualism. Educators and social scientists worry about the panorama of culture-contact problems, but also look optimistically towards new, richer ways of learning being developed by native educators.

I close this exploration of native educator roles with one such optimistic example of a setting in which both community elders and professional teachers are finding complementary new educational roles involving the language, content, and learning-teaching processes of the two cultures making up their children's lives. In this setting, the 1983 resolution (83-18) of the Inuit Circumpolar Conference General Assembly--"that our educational systems are to prepare our children for life based on values and skills from the Inuit culture and the western culture"--is put into action. In northern Alaska, the Inupiaq qargi--the community house where youth traditionally went to listen to and learn from elders--is being re-established on a trial basis as a parallel to the modern formal school. This is a response to almost 50 years of assimilationist education which has resulted in a generation of children who are virtual strangers to the native culture. In the new qargi, in native language, a young professionally trained native teacher "would work side by side with the elders of each community, thereby allowing the teacher to absorb both the knowledge possessed by the elder(s), and the manner in which the children were taught. Skills learned in school, such as mathematics, could be applied in the qari, where children are building sleds or boats, for example" (MacLean in Curwin 1986: 21). Here, as isumaqsayuq and ilisayuq meet, native educators are in fact creating new cultural roles for themselves.

Conclusion

Optimism for the future of native education in Canada is difficult in light of overwhelming failures for which the evidence is all too familiar (e.g., high rates of school drop-out, language loss, political confrontation, drug abuse, crime, and suicide). Perhaps we can take some hope from growing attention over recent years to the idea and dynamics of native-nonnative cultural brokerage (Brody 1975, Paine 1971, 1977, Simard 1983, Williamson 1974, Wyatt 1978-79), and from at least a few successful educational examples (e.g. Jobidan 1984, Kleinfeld 1979, Macias 1987, Stairs 1988a, Wyatt-Benuyon 1986).

The first feature of these successes is some movement from cultural inclusion to cultural base in the conceptualization and implementation of native education. As illustrated in Figure 1, this movement rests on the progressive incorporation of schools into the native cultural context --from the language and content aspects discussed in the previous article to the process aspects (ecological, social, and cognitive) explored in this article. Some next steps in native educational research and development might focus on the most apparent correlates of this progress:

						BROAD CULT- URAL BASE
					EXPAND- ING CULT- URAL BASE	cognitive process
				NARROW CULT- URAL BASE	social process	social process
			CULT- URAL INCLU- SION	ecological context	ecological context	ecological context
		LIMITED CULT- URAL INCLU- SION	content material	content material	content material	content material
NO NATIVE CULT- URAL INCLU- SION	native language	native language+	native language++	native language +++	native language ++++
		LABELS IN NL	ORGAN- ZES IN NL	COMMU- NICATES IN NL	THINKS ABOUT IN NL

Figure 1 The Cultural Basis of Learning and Teaching in Native Education

NL = Native Language

- emerging oral and written linguistic forms (in both native languages and English; see Burnaby 1985 Leavitt this volume, Shearwood 1987, Stairs, 1985) as cultural bridges;

- developing native educator roles (see above) as culture brokers between native and Eurocanadian ways of knowing.

The second feature of success in native education may be the converse side of cultural brokerage--attention to and incorporation of certain native ways of learning into mainstream formal education. There is a current malaise over the decontextualized nature of much North American schooling (e.g. Cole 1988, Resnick 1987), and a search for more socially functional models of learning (e.g. Bruner 1986, Lave 1988, Rogoff 1982). The native traditions of contextualized and shared learning may offer clues for schooling directed towards more effective living in our environment and with each other (Stairs 1988c). Canadian education has much to gain as well as to give in brokerage with native cultures. I suggest in closing that genuine two-way brokerage between native culture and formal schooling validates native ways of learning, response to urgent mainstream needs, and is our collective path to success in native education.

Note
I thank the Inuit and other native people with whom I have worked for involving me in the instructive cultural brokerage on which this article is based. Preparation of the article was stimulated by TESL students in native language and education courses at Concordia University during the summers of 1987 and 1988.

References

Annahatak, B. (1985).
Philosophy of Inuit Education. Paper Prepared for Symposium '85 on Inuit Education, Kuujjuaq, Q.C: Kativik School Board.

Briggs, J. L. (1979).
Aspects of Inuit Value Socialization. Ottawa: National Museum of Man Mercury Series.

Briggs, J.L. (1983).
Le modéle traditionnel l'éducation chez les Inuit. Recherches Amérindiennes au Québec 13: 13-25.

Brody, H. (1975).
The Peoples' Land. Harmondsworth: Penguin.

Bruner, J. (1986).
Actual Minds, Possible Worlds. Cambridge, Mass.: Harvard University Press.

Bullivant, B. M. (1984).
Pluralism: Cultural Maintenance and Evolution. Clevedon: Multilingual Matters.

Burnaby, B. (1982).
Languages and Their Roles in Native Education. Toronto: Ontario Institute for Studies in Education.

Burnaby, B. (ed.) (1985).
Promoting Native Writing Systems in Canada. Toronto: Ontario Institute for Studies in Education Press.

Cole, M. (1988).
A Cultural Theory of Learning and Development: Implications for Educational Research and Practice. Paper Presented to the American Educational Research Association, New Orleans.

Cummins, J. (1983).
Heritage Language Education. Toronto: Ministry of Education.

Curwin, K. (186).
Edna Maclean of the Alaska Native Language Centre: Traditional Qargi Can Link Old Ways to Western School System. Inuit (I.C.C), 20-21.

Harrison, B. G. (1981).
Informal Learning among Yup'ik Eskimos: An Ethnographic Study of one Alaskan Village. Doctoral Dissertation, University of Oregon.

Jobifdon, O. (ed.) (1984).
Successes in Indian Education: A Sharing. A Conference to Assess the State of the Art. Vancouver, B.C.: British Columbia Ministry of Education.

Kleinfeld, J. (1979).
Eskimo School on the Andrefsky: A Study of Effective Bicultural Education. New York: Praeger.

Lave, J. (1988).
Cognition in Practice. New York: Cambridge University Press.

Macias, J. (1987).
The Hidden Curriculum of Papago Teachers: American Indian Strategies for Mitigating Cultural Discontinuity in Early Schooling. In G. Spindler and L. Spindler (eds.), Interpretive Ethnography of Education, 45-56. Hillsdale, NJ: Erlbaum.

Modiano, N. (1974-1975).
Using Native Instructional Patterns for Teacher Training: A Chiapas Experiment. In R. Troike and N. Modiano (eds.), Proceedings of the First Inter-American Conference on Bilingual Education, 76-87. Mexico City.

Nappaaluk, M. (c. 1985).
Qimminuulignajut ilumiutartangit (The Dog Book). Dorval: Kativik School Board.

Paine, R. (ed.) (1971).
Patrons and Brokers in the East Arctic. St. John's Memorial University of Newfoundland, Institute of Social and Economic Research.

Paine, R. (ed.) (1977).
The White Arctic: Anthropological Essays on Tutelage and Ethnicity. St. John's: Memorial University of Newfoundland.

Philips, S. U. (1983).
The Invisible Culture: Communication in the Classroom and Community on the Warm Spring's Indian Reserve. New York: Longman.

Piddington, R. (1951).
An Anthropologist's Viewpoint. In J.A. Lauwarys and N. Hans (eds.), 34-43, The Yearbook of Education. London: Evans.

Resnick, L. B. (1987).
Learning in School and Out. Educational Researcher 16: 13-20.

Rogoff, B. (1982).
Integrating Context and Cognitive development. In M. E. Lamb and A. L. Brown (eds.), Advances in Developmental Psychology, Volume 2, 45-56. Hillsdale, N.J.: Erlbaum.

Scollon, R. and Scollon, S. K. (1981).
Narrative, Literacy, and Face in Interethnic Communication. Norwood, N.J.: Ablex.

Shearwood, P. (1987).
Literacy among the Aboriginal Peoples of the Northwest Territories. Canadian Modern Language Review 43: 630-642.

Simard, J. J. (1983).
Par-dela entre le blanc et le mal: Rapports identitaires et colonialisme au pays des Inuit. Sociologie et Sociétes 15: 55-71.

Sindell, P. (1987).
Some Discontinuities in the Enculturation of Mistassini Cree Children. In G. D. Spindler (ed.), Education and Cultural Process: Anthropological Approaches, 23-34. Prospect Heights: Waveland.

Stairs, A. (1985).
La viabilité des langues autochtones et le rôle de l'écrit: l'expérience de l'inuktitut au Nouveau Québec. Recherches Amérindiennes au Québec 15: 23-34.

Stairs, A. (1988a).
Beyond Cultural Inclusion: An Inuit Example of Indigenous Educational Development. In T. Skutnabb-Kangas and J. Cummins (eds.), Minority Education, 34-53. Clevedon: Multilingual Matters.

Stairs, A. (1988b).
Native Models for Learning. Educational Researcher 17: 23-32.

Stairs, A. (1988c).
The Professional Development of Native Educators: Context, Culture, and Language. TESL Canada Journal 5: 34-45.

Wenzel, G. (in press).
I Was Once Independent. Anthropologica.

Williamson, R. G. (1974).
Eskimos Underground. Upssala: Upssala University Press.

Wolcott, H. (1982).
The Anthropology of Learning. Anthropology and Education Quarterly 13: 83-108.

Wyatt, J. (1978-1979).
Native Involvement in Curriculum Development: The Native Teacher as Culture Broker. Interchange 8: 7-28.

Wyatt-Benyon, J. (1986).
The Mt. Currie Indian Community School: Innovation and Endurance. In H. McCue (ed.), Selected Papers from the First Mokakit Conference, 34-45. Vancouver: Mokakit/University of British Columbia.

LANGUAGE NEEDS AND CHARACTERISTICS OF SASKATCHEWAN INDIAN AND METIS STUDENTS: IMPLICATIONS FOR EDUCATORS

Mary Heit and Heather Blair

Introduction
This paper will examine the language characteristics of Indian and Metis students in Saskatchewan and the nature of the school programs that are presently available to meet their language needs. It will go on to discuss dialects, the characteristics of Indigenous English, and the issues involved in the teaching of standard English to dialect speaking students. Finally, the implications of the above for education will be drawn.

The Cultural and Linguistic Spectrum
A comprehensive overview of the Saskatchewan Indigenous population will reveal that it is extremely varied: culturally, linguistically, geographically, socially, and economically. For the purposes of this paper, the focus will be on the linguistic diversity of Saskatchewan Indian and Metis students. The following six cultural and linguistic groups are indigenous to present day Saskatchewan:
- Cree
- Saulteaux
- Dene
- Assiniboine
- Dakota
- Metis

The majority of speakers of Indigenous languages in Saskatchewan speak an Algonkian language. The Cree and Saulteaux languages belong to the Algonkian language family. There are three dialects of Cree spoken in Saskatchewan, with the majority of people speaking the "y" dialect, or Plains Cree. The "n" dialect or Swampy Cree is spoken by the people in Cumberland House, while the "th" dialect or Bush Cree is spoken by the people in the La Ronge Area. Reserves and communities were Algonkian languages are spoken are found in south-central Saskatchewan and in the northern parklands and bush areas.

The second language family represented in Saskatchewan is the Siouan language family, comprised of the Dakota and Assiniboine (Nakota) languages. Speakers of these languages are much fewer in number, and reserves where they may be found are in the south-eastern areas of the province, with the exception of Wahpeton reserve, which is just north of Prince Albert, and Mosquito reserve near North Battleford.

Finally, the Dene language spoken by the Chipewyan people of the far northern part of the province belongs to the Athapaskan language family. These three language families are as different from one another as Slavic languages are from Romance languages.

The Metis people constitute a separate cultural group as well, and will be found in every area of the province. Depending on their backgrounds, Metis people may speak any of the above languages. In addition, a French-Cree dialect called "Michif" was once quite widespread amongst Metis people of French-Cree descent, and is still spoken by some people in certain areas of the province. The influence of Michif is now noticeable in the spoken English of many Metis people.

Of course, speakers of the Indigenous languages are no longer found only on reserves or in Metis communities, but now live in every major urban center in Saskatchewan and in many rural centers as well. Moreover, most Indian and Metis people now speak English as their first language or in addition to their Indigenous language, so that a look at the language characteristics of Saskatchewan Indian and Metis students reveals a very broad spectrum. Teachers in Saskatchewan schools, depending in which area of the province they are teaching, can expect to encounter Indian or Metis students who may:

1. *be monolingual in an Indigenous language:*
   This could be considered as one end of the spectrum. Most Indian or Metis students who begin school monolingual in an Indigenous language live in northern Saskatchewan and are Cree or Dene speakers. Teachers in the Northern Lights

School Division would be likely to encounter such students, depending in which community they are teaching. As well, many members of the older generation of Indian or Metis people speak only an Indigenous language.

2. *be monolingual in English:*
   This could be considered the opposite end of the spectrum. It is frequently the case for many Indian students in large urban centers who have had a great deal of exposure to English and whose families have lived away from the reserve for some time. As well, many Metis students are monolingual in English, depending upon their backgrounds.
3. *speak a dialect of English:*
   Many Indian and Metis people speak a variety of English that differs from what is termed "standard" English, the variety of English generally utilized in schools. This is a fact which is just beginning to be recognized by researchers and educators, and will be discussed in more detail later in this paper.
4. *be bilingual in an Indigenous language and English:*
   Many Indian and Metis people in northern Saskatchewan, many of the older generation in southern Saskatchewan, and those younger people who come from homes or reserves where the Indian language is still spoken and maintained may be active bilinguals.
5. *speak an Indigenous language and some degree of English:*
   In other words, the students' command of English is not sufficient for them to be termed "bilingual". These students likely come from backgrounds similar to those described for bilingual students.
6. *speak English or a dialect of English and some degree of an Indigenous language:*
   Once again, the command of the Indigenous language may not be sufficient for the student to be termed "bilingual". Perhaps the student understands the Indigenous language but speaks very little of it (receptive bilingual). This is frequently the pattern in situations where only the grandparents speak the Indigenous language, parents are bilingual, and children speak only English.

The message for educators is that not all Indian and Metis students can be lumped into one category as far as language characteristics are concerned, but that, in fact, there exists a very broad range of linguistic characteristics and corresponding needs for Indian and Metis students across Saskatchewan which need to be taken into account by educators.

Statistics and Demography

In Saskatchewan today many existing programs using curricula and methodologies designed for first language standard English speakers have not worked very well for Indian and Metis children and adults. According to the standardized instruments, Indian and Metis children are falling behind their classmates to the extent of two to three years. While undoubtedly there are many out of school factors as well which contribute to age grade displacement and/or high attrition and limited graduation rates, this paper focuses on the issues of language differences, inappropriate methodologies and programming, and teacher awareness about language as key in-school factors which educators need to examine.

According to the 1981 census, there were 54,188 Treaty Indians in Saskatchewan and 45,000 Metis, the latter being a conservative estimate. This is about 10% of the population of Saskatchewan. In northern Saskatchewan (the area covered by the Northern Lights School Division), there were 25,000 people living in 44 communities and reserves in 1981. The population is very young, with almost 40% being under the age of 15 years and 61% under the age of 25 years. In the 1981 census, 39% of the national Indian population was under the age of 15 years. The increase in the Indian and Metis population of school age children relative to the non-Native population is worth noting if, as is suggested by the Svenson report, by the year 2001 Indian and Metis children will comprise 45.7% of the entire school population in Saskatchewan.

The message for educators is obvious. For example, 25 of the 32 provincially funded schools in northern Saskatchewan are situated in Metis communities where English is spoken as a second language. A Mississippi Broadcasting Corporation survey of 852 northern residents in 1984 found that 25.7% of those surveyed spoke or understood Dene, 80.28% spoke or understood Cree, and 96.01% spoke or understood English. Hence, many Northerners have some degree of facility with more than one language. Of the 68 Indian bands in the province with federal or band controlled schools, 28 out of 38 responding on a survey indicated that between 10 and 100 percent of their pupils speak an Indian language as the main language at home. Burnaby's (1982) thesis supports this with an extrapolation from the 1971 census which suggests that half of the people who considered themselves to be of Indian or Inuit ancestry in Canada reported that their mother tongue was an Indian language. Although we presently do not have a precise number, these figures certainly bring up the question of how many of the Indian and Metis children in this province are from second language homes.

Add to the picture as well the fact that a considerable number of Indian and Metis people have recently (within the last 10-15 years) become urban dwellers. In 1984, 66% of the Treaty Indians in Saskatchewan lived in rural areas and 34% lived in urban centers. Nationally this is the largest percentage living off reserve next to British Columbia. About half of Treaty Indian students are now being educated in provincial schools. Figures for percentages of urban Metis dwellers are not available but likely they resemble those of Treaty Indians.

1981 CENSUS: SASKATCHEWAN

Treaty Indians	54,188
Metis and Non-Status	45,000
Total	94,000+
	(10% of provincial total)

Northern Saskatchewan	25,000
40% under 15 years	
61% under 25 years	
(Compares to National Indian Population from last census: 39% under 15 years of age)	

Svenson Report: by the year 2001, 45.7% of school age children in Saskatchewan will be Indian and Metis children.

Demographic Change: in 1984, 66% of Treaty people in Saskatchewan lived on the reserve and 34% lived off reserve.

Bilingualism
   1. Missinipi Broadcasting Corporation Survey, 1984

   852 residents in 44 communities
   Languages spoken:

Dene	Cree	English
25.7%	80.28%	96.01%

2. Northern Lights School Division:
 25/32 schools were in communities where English is spoken as a second language. A great many of the community members are bilingual Cree and Dene speakers.
3. Indian bands:
 There are 68 bands in Saskatchewan. 28/36 responded on a survey that 10-100% of their children speak an Indian language as their mother tongue.

Nature of Language Programs Available for Indian and Metis Students

Obviously, linguistic and cultural distributions and patterns of language used are rapidly being altered by the migration of Indian and Metis people to the cities. Indian or Metis children who may have quite recently moved from a reserve or community with the kind of language composition we have talked about are entering urban schools where the language of instruction is English, where all programming is designed for first language English speakers, and where they are assessed and evaluated with the same language proficiency instruments and measures of "intelligence" as their first language English speaking peers. As educators in this province, we need to examine these trends and the implications that they hold for all educational institutions and language programming.

A look at the types of language programs available in Saskatchewan provincial schools reveals that Indian and Metis students receive their language education via the "regular" program route--that of English-only instruction. This is the case even in schools where Indian or Metis children form the majority and where their first language upon entry into school is not English. Out of 251 provincial schools responding to a survey conducted by the Saskatchewan Indian Languages Institute, only 17 offered instruction in an Indigenous language in their school programs. Twenty-five out of fifty-three band-controlled schools and fifteen out of twenty-three federal schools responding to the same survey indicated that they offered instruction in an Indigenous language. No schools offered bilingual programs, and Indian and Metis students do not qualify for English as a second language (ESL) programs under the terms of present funding structures.

We have seen that Indian and Metis students possess a wide range of language characteristics and corresponding needs. Yet language programs presently in place in provincial schools do not reflect this fact, and hence are likely not meeting the needs of students who begin school speaking an Indigenous language or possessing a degree of bilinguality in English and Indigenous language. This is particularly true of northern Saskatchewan, where there are obvious implications for administrators, teachers, language program design, and materials development.

Immersion and Submersion Programs

Many educators, when discussing language programming for Indian and Metis students, will make comments like: "If English-speaking children can learn to speak French in French immersion programs, why can't Indian and Metis children learn to speak English in English-only programs?" The assumption is that the situation is the same for English-speaking and Indian or Metis children in both programs. In reality, the situations are very different, as we shall see.

The term "submersion" has been used to describe the type of language program in which Indian and Metis children most commonly receive their education. This type of program has not met with a great deal of success as far as the language education of Indian and Metis students is concerned. Cohen and Swain (1976) make the comparison between minority children in "submersion" English and majority children in "immersion" French. Burnaby (1976) and Toohey (1985) make a similar comparison for Indian and Metis students in English "submersion" and Anglo children in French "immersion". There are many things about the details of these programs that differ, but let us look just briefly at the overall contexts in which they are set.

1. For Indian and Metis parents there is generally little opportunity for input into the curriculum and even less for any decisions affecting school policy.
2. Indian and Metis people did not ask for English-only instruction; it was imposed from within.
3. There are few Indian language or bilingual instruction classes available as options to the English program.
4. In contrast to French immersion, English-only programming was never regarded as an experiment to be monitored, assessed and evaluated prior to policies being made. Rather, English-only programs were tactics for assimilating the Indian or Metis child, with full intentions of being carried through without question.
5. There is no evidence that there has been any sincere concern on the part of decision makers that the Indigenous languages be maintained. Rather, they have been viewed historically as impediments to the school progress of Indian and Metis children and treated as liabilities rather than as assets.

Summary of the Differences Between French Immersion and English Submersion

1. French immersion teachers are all bilingual and able to communicate in the child's first language if necessary; whereas most English submersion teachers speak English only.
2. In the French immersion class, the students' first language may be used until they are ready to use the second language. Children are not expected to have perfect pronunciation in the target language, nor to have a full grasp of all its structures and lexicon. It is accepted that they will have an accent, and errors are expected and tolerated.
3. With the immersion program, English language arts are introduced at grade 2 or 3 and by the middle years, content subjects are also taught in the first language; in submersion, instruction in the Indian language is rare, and its use as a medium of instruction is non-existent.
4. Teaching material is more readily available for teaching French as a second language (FSL) to urban children than for teaching English as a second language (ESL) to Indian and Metis children.
5. The English language has prestige, as it is the language of power in the larger society and in the world; the Indian child's first language is likely to not be highly valued by schools and may be under attack in the community.
6. English and French languages and cultures are more closely related than English and Indigenous languages and cultures.
7. While immersion students are expected to learn only an appreciation of French ways, Indian and Metis children are expected to become assimilated.
8. For the middle class child, French immersion is a publicly appreciated goal and an educational extra; for the Indian and Metis child, English is an expected minimum and an economic necessity.
9. French immersion programs have a considerable research base in second language learning theory

and teaching practice and their success has been well-documented. Submersion programs, on the other hand, are a result of public ignorance and neglect regarding the language education of minority language children.

10. Parents have control over and put pressure on educational authorities which introduce French immersion, but Indian and Metis parents do not have control over those bringing in submersion. These programs are imposed by outside, sometimes hostile, authorities.
11. Children in French immersion are segregated linguistically so that they are "all in the same boat", unlike the Indian or Metis child who, in an integrated classroom, is likely to be one of very few learning English as a second language or dialect and is surrounded by often less than sympathetic classmates whose first language is English.
12. The English child experiencing difficulty in French immersion may drop out and can switch to an English program without penalty, while the Indian or Metis child has no such educational retreat and will likely be diagnosed as having a "language problem" or being in need of remedial education if he or she has difficulty in the English-only program.
13. The French immersion teacher has been trained in second language learning principles and teaching practices, and knows that the English speaking child will eventually master both the second language and the subject matter. This is not always the case for teachers of Indian and Metis children.
14. There is a double standard that is applied to the child's achievement: "People applaud a majority group child when he can say a few words in the minority language and yet they impatiently demand more English from the minority group child" (Cohen and Swain 1976: 51)

Obviously, the situation for ESL Indian or Metis students in English-only programs is very different from the situation of majority language children in French immersion programs. Research shows

(Cummins 1981) that minority language children will do well academically when both languages continue to develop, when the first language is used as a medium of instruction for at least art of the school day, and where the language program of the school is supported by parents and community. Yet, at the present time in Saskatchewan provincial schools, various bilingual program options have not been explored.

"But My Students All Speak English": The Nature of Dialects
Most teachers in provincial schools, excluding those in the Northern Lights School Division, will encounter Indian or Metis students who may no longer speak an Indigenous language. As was pointed out earlier, there are many Indian or Metis students who are indeed fluent in "standard" English. However, a good many Indian and Metis students who are learning English as a second language and who come from homes where the Indigenous language is still spoken may run into difficulties at school. This is because it may appear to teachers that these students have a sufficient grasp of the English language to succeed in school, when in reality they may need a great deal more exposure to intensive language teaching of a communicative, meaningful nature (Toohey 1982).

As well, a good many Indian and Metis students speak a fully-fledged dialect of English that is the result of the influence of the Indigenous language or mother tongue upon the English language. It is the nature of dialects and of "Indigenous English" in particular that is the focus of this portion of the paper.

Frequently, when students speak a type of English that may differ from "standard English", teachers may view their language as problematic or as exhibiting deficiencies or errors of some sort. There is a need for educators to understand the nature of dialects and of second language learning, and to counter the deficit view with one that explains and accepts the existence of difference within a language and where these come from.

What is Dialect?
The research in dialectology can be summarized by the following points:

1. The term dialect refers to varieties of the same language. Dialects are not different languages, but are variations of a single language, but are variations of a single language, exhibiting varying degrees of differences in the areas of pronunciation, grammar, vocabulary, and discourse patterns (more on this later).

2. The differences between these varieties of language exist mainly at the spoken or oral level. Speakers of different dialects of a language, even if they can barely understand one another, will still all be able to understand the standard written form of that language if they have become literate. Standard forms of written language have been arrived at chiefly by the invention of writing, which tends to standardize a language (usually the language or dialect of the dominant group of the society) into an unchanging or permanent form. Spoken language, on the other hand, is constantly changing, and exhibits differences on the personal, group, and regional levels. What we term "standard" English varies in its spoken form from Britain to Canada, for example, and even within Canada.
3. Dialects are a universal phenomenon of language. All major and widespread languages have dialects. There are many dialects of English, for example, which exist around the globe. The more widespread a language is, geographically and socially, the more dialects of it there will be.
4. Dialects can have varying degrees of mutual intelligibility. For example, speakers of what can broadly be termed "Canadian English" may be unable at first to understand speakers of Jamaican English. As well, it is likely less difficult for speakers of Canadian English to understand speakers of Black English, and even easier to understand speakers of American or British English.
5. The standard form of a language refers to that variety or dialect of a language which is usually used in print and which is normally taught in the schools. It is this variety of language that is generally associated with the highly educated people in a society, that is the most prestigious or socially acceptable, and that is heard on television or radio.
6. Dialects are a result of regional and social distinctions, and can reflect as well the influences of a people's first language or mother tongue. Dialects can be the result of geographic separation, such as Canadian English from British English, and they

also can be a reflection of social class. Working class people will often speak differently from middle and upper class people, for example. As well, when speakers of one language learn another language, to the extent of they no longer speaking their mother tongue, its influence (called an accent) will be felt for at least three generations, and will frequently result in the permanent formation of a new dialect. The case of many Indian and Metis people in Saskatchewan is an example of this, where, in three generations, young people have switched to English. However, the influence of the Indigenous language is still noticeable in the features of the dialect.

7. Research shows that dialects of English are legitimate, systematic, and rule-governed. Dialects are languages. They have their own internal logic and do not constitute "broken", sub-standard, quaint, or deficient forms of language. They are fully capable of expressing all the needs and intentions of their speakers in the milieu in which they have evolved. The variations from the standard which they exhibit are not haphazard, but occur consistently and logically. Hence, these variations should not be viewed as "errors" in need of correction.

8. Many speakers of non-standard dialects also have command of the standard dialect when the situation warrants it. This ability is known as diglossia or code-switching, and is a common phenomenon in societies where standard and non-standard dialects co-exist. All literate speakers of Black English, for example, will be able to read, write, and understand standard English to varying degrees. Many will also speak standard English in certain formal or employment situations when it is warranted. In their homes or with their friends however, they may choose to speak Black English. The same phenomenon holds true for many Indian and Metis peoples. It is the element of individual choice here that is crucial.

9. A dialect can be a reflection of individual or group identity. All of us speak the dialect of the group

into which we are born and/or with which we identify. The way we speak is very closely tied to our sense of self. For many people, it is a sign of group solidarity, identity, or sense of belonging. Hence, the inseparable relationship between language, culture, and personality. Speakers of non-standard dialects who choose to speak their dialects rather than the standard form, likely do so out of feelings of personal or group identity. If a speaker of Black English, for example, were to attempt to speak standard English with his or her peers, it is likely that such a person would be ridiculed or rejected by his/her social group. Thus, attempts to change or to eradicate features of dialect can often be met by resistance or will be perceived as threatening to individual or to group identity.
10. Certain non-standard dialects can evoke negative attitudes on the part of listeners. It is not the non-standard dialects per say that constitute a problems, but rather the attitudes that many people hold towards them and hence towards the people who speak them. Certain dialects are associated with prestige and wealth for example, while others are associated with illiteracy or ignorance. Research shows that listeners, including teachers, make unconscious judgements about the people based on the way that they speak.

Indigenous English

There is increasing research evidence supporting the theory that varieties of English spoken by many Indian or Metis people are in fact, dialects of English. Undoubtedly, there are many of these dialects, because of the broad range of geographic, social, cultural and linguistic backgrounds of Indian and Metis peoples. In this paper, the term "Indigenous English" is used as a blanket term to describe the varieties of English spoken by Indian and Metis peoples.

As with all dialects, there are consistent, regular, and logical differences that exist between standard English and Indigenous English. Note the use of the term "differences" as opposed to "deficiencies". A great deal of damage has been done to Indian and Metis students who have been misdiagnosed as having language or learning problems due to differences in their spoken English that have been misunderstood by educators, who, through no fault of their own, have not been trained in these areas.

The differences between Indigenous English and standard English are not as obvious as the differences that exist between standard English and Black English or Jamaican English, for example. This could have two consequences, one positive and one negative:

1. differences are not so great so as to interfere significantly with meaning or communication in the classroom;
2. however, teachers may not realize that the differences are features of dialect or natural consequences of learning English as a second language, and may attempt to correct or change the speech of their students rather than focusing on the meaning of what their students are saying.

Differences between standard English and Indigenous English exist at the following four levels, as they do for all dialects (note that most of the following examples compare Cree and English, since this is the area in which the most research pertinent to Saskatchewan has been conducted and is available):

1. *Differences in Pronunciation*
a. The intonation, emphasis and stress patterns of Indigenous languages differ from those of English. In English, we convey our feelings or our attitudes to what we say by our tone of voice and the stress we place on words. We emphasize certain words by pronouncing them more loudly, for example. In Cree, emphasis can also be conveyed by the order of words in a sentence. In Dene, emphasis and speaker feelings towards what is being said can be conveyed by the use of a particular grammatical form. As well, emphasis, stress, and intonation sometimes occur in different places in phrases and sentences. Speakers of Indigenous languages unconsciously bring their stresses and intonation patterns to the task of speaking English, and this contributes to their having an identifiable accent.

b. There are sounds in English that do not exist in Cree, and vice versa. When speakers of Cree who are learning to speak English encounter a sound in English that does not exist in Cree, they are likely to pronounce it with the closest sound that exists to it in their own language. This will also contribute to their having an identifiable accent. There is no /v/ or /s/ ("sh") sound in Cree, for example, as there is in English. The closest sound in Cree would be /b/ or /s/; hence, Cree children learning English will say "ballentine" instead of "valentine", or "sue" instead of "shoe". Similarly, the closest sound in Cree to the /j/ and the /c/ (ch) sounds in English are "dz" and "ts", respectively, so that, for example, "jam" may be pronounced "dzam" and "church" as "tsurts". This is a logical result of the contrasts between the two languages, and is not evidence of a speech defect or language disability. Obviously, students will need more exposure to and practice with the sounds of English that do not occur in the Indigenous language.

c. There is no distinction in Cree between what are termed voiced and unvoiced stops: /p/ and /b/, /d/, and /t/, /g/ and /k/. For example, in English, it makes a difference in meaning if we say "pit" or "bit". In Cree, it makes no difference in meaning if the word for "seven" is pronounced "tepagohp" or "tepakop". Many Cree people who speak English as a second language or dialect will not differentiate between these sounds in their speech. They may pronounce "things" as "thinks", for example. This can be a source of difficulty in their learning to read if too much emphasis is placed on phonics as a reading strategy.

d. Some vowels exist in English which do not exist in Cree or are pronounced differently. This leads to such differences as saying "melk" for "milk"; "earli" for "early"; or "tuh" for "two". In Cree too, it makes a difference in meaning if a vowel is held for a long or short duration. For example, "nipa" means "to kill" and "nipa" (the /a/ is held longer) means "to sleep". However, vowel duration is not a significant feature of English pronunciation.

e. The Cree language has vowels occurring at the end of many words. As well, there are no nasal sounds in Cree, such as the "-ing" ending which is so common in English. As a result, final consonants are sometimes omitted in English by Cree second language or dialect speakers: "walkin'" or "goin'", for example.

2. *Differences in Grammar*

a. In English grammar or syntax, word order is quite rigid. We cannot say "The dog see I" or "I the dog see", for example. We must say "I see the dog" to be grammatically correct. In Cree, grammaticality is not conveyed by word order. It is possible to say "Niwapamaw atim" or "Atim niwapamaw". The emphasis changes, but both utterances are grammatical. ("Atim" means "dog" and "niwapamaw" means "I see").

b. English is a highly irregular language, as all English teachers can attest! All dialects of English tend to regularize the irregularities they encounter in standard English. Indigenous English is no exception. For example, if we have "shirt" and "shirts", why can't we have "pant" and "pants" instead of "a pair of pants"? Many Cree people thus will say "a pants" for a "a pair of pants" or "pantses" for the plural. Similarly, "woman" is often pluralized as "womans". The use of the word "scissors" is also irregular in English. "These scissors are dull" is correct in standard English, even when we are referring to only one pair of scissors. Cree English speakers will show that they mean the singular by saying "this scissors is dull", which is only logical. Many verbs in English are irregular as well, especially the common ones like "to see", "to do", "to be", and "to have". Speakers of dialects of English will regularize these verbs by such constructions as "I seen", "I done", "I been", or "I gots". This sometimes happens in Indigenous English as well.

The verb "to be" is used differently in such constructions as "Don't be doing that, my boy", for example.

c. As in many Indigenous languages, Cree classifies things according to whether they are animate or inanimate, and not according to a gender that is masculine, feminine, or neuter as in English. Thus Cree students learning English will frequently use "he" when they mean "she". Similarly, the word in Cree for "husband" and "wife" is the same, and may be translated simply as "spouse". Hence many Cree ESL speakers unfamiliar with the word "spouse" since it is rather uncommon, will say "wife" when they mean "husband". This is a result of the differences between the languages and should not be viewed as an inability to discern the difference between masculine and feminine!

d. Some dialect speakers (a feature of Michif) will use inflection to convey a question: "Are you goint to the show?" or "Can you lend me some money?" becomes "You're going to the show?" and "You'll lend me some money?"

3. *Differences in Vocabulary*

a. As is the case for many languages, color terms and many other concepts as well, in Indigenous languages are not directly translatable into English. For example, there is one word for "brown" and "green" in Cree which might be translated as "ear-colored" in English. This is just one example of how language reflects the way in which different cultures classify or view the world.

b. There are many expressions in Indigenous English that differ from standard English. These are some examples: "Give me cuts" (when someone cuts into a lineup of people), "Close the lights" (instead of "shut off" or "put out"), "Get off the way" (instead of "Get out of the way"), "Can I camp over at your place?" (instead of "can I stay" or "can I sleep at your place"), "We really suffered him" (instead of "we really made him suffer" or "we really teased him"), "Those kids are always meaning on him" (instead of "being mean to him"), "You did good" (instead of "you did well"), "I don't know what do, me" (could be an influence from French), "I was just tired" ("just" used in the sense of "very" or "really"), "He was sick, but" or "I don't have any money, but", (This is a feature of Metchif, when "but" is used to convey the meaning of "because"; in other words, "He couldn't come because he was sick" or "I can't go because I don't have any money"), "I don't talk Cree" (instead of "I don't speak Cree"), "She plays all the time, bing" (a noun placed at the end of the sentence for emphasis), "When are you going to come visit?" or "I'm going to come visit you soon" (different usage of the term "to visit"), "Who's keeping the kids?" (instead of "who's looking after the kids?"), "Look at her little small feet!" ("little, small" are used together to describe something that is cute).

4. *Differences in Discourse*
a. There are differences at the discourse level as well, which is the level at which sentences are put together or connected in written or spoken language.
b. There is evidence that people who speak an Indigenous language tend to organize and tie together their English speech or writing in the same way that they do the Indigenous language. For example, some research indicates that speakers of Athapaskan languages such as Dene organize their narratives in two's and four's rather than in three's (beginning, middle, and end), which is typical of English discourse.
c. Rules for emphasizing ideas, for introducing topics, for sequencing, and for ending discourse differ between English and Indigenous languages. When speakers of Indigenous languages unconsciously transfer these rules to English, it can result in the feeling on the part of English listeners that their ideas are not coherent, or stated well. This happens as well to other speaker of languages very different from English when they try to convey their thoughts in spoken or written discourse.

The whole issue of dialectical differences between Indigenous languages and English, particularly in the area of discourse analysis, is a very recent area of study that requires a great deal more research. However, the differences noted above are sufficient reason for educators to pause and reflect upon the role of language in the education of Indian and Metis students.

Teacher Attitudes to Student Language

Before going on to discuss the implications of the above, it is necessary to acknowledge the importance of teacher attitudes to students' language. The lack of knowledge about second language learning and the nature of dialects has led and will continue to lead to misunderstandings and miseducation of Indian and Metis students when language differences are interpreted as language deficiencies, or when they lead to the formation of stereotypes or misjudgments of someone's ability on the basis of his/her spoken language. Many teachers continue to see their role as one of correcting the students' spoken English to conform to "standard English". This has been the history of language education for Indian and Metis students. In light of the fact that dialects are languages and that language, culture, and personality are intimately interrelated, to "correct" someone's language is tantamount to saying that the culture or person is not acceptable. The long-term effects of constant correction, focus on form rather than on content, and non-acceptance of students' language likely contribute to the silence which many Indian and Metis students retreat to in classrooms and to the high attrition rates of which we are all aware.

It is a documented research fact that teachers' values, beliefs, and expectations about students' achievement levels are conveyed to students' at an unconscious level, resulting in the "self-fulfilling prophecy" (Brophy and Good 1977). Teacher attitudes to students' language are similarly conveyed. Students who do not speak standard Canadian English may internalize the message from their teachers and from the larger society that they themselves are not acceptable because their language is not considered acceptable. This could have three possible results:

1. students may become ashamed of or uncomfortable with their speech, which will have an effect upon self-concept;
2. students may conclude that the teacher doesn't like them;
3. students may withdraw or rebel, confirming the teacher's original expectation that they have a "problem".

The problem then may not be with the child or the child's language ("blaming the victim"), but rather the teachers' attitudes might be what is producing the barrier. This in fact was the decision reached in a landmark court decision in the United States in 1978 (Freeman 1982, Smitherman 1981) in the Ann Arbor Schools case. The judge ruled that the language of the students (in this case, Black English) was indeed a language and not improper English, and that the unconscious negative attitudes of teachers to Black English were creating language barriers that could be a contributing reason for the students experiencing difficulty with reading.

1. An attitude towards a language is a judgement of its worth.
2. People make judgements all the time, usually at an unconscious level, about a person's intelligence, ethnicity, personality, or educational level from the way that he or she speaks. Studies have shown, for example, that teachers will rate speakers of standard English as most acceptable and most likely to succeed in school (Freeman 1982).
3. As we have seen in our discussion of dialects, judgements concerning the superiority or inferiority of dialects are not scientific or based on linguistic proof. Rather, they are made on social grounds and reflect our own individual or ethnic biases.

Implications for Educators
1. The nature of dialects and of second language learning, the principles of cross-cultural education, and a knowledge of Indian and Metis history and contemporary issues have not been properly understood by many teachers and administrators in Saskatchewan. This is partly because Indian and Metis students are relative newcomers to provincial school systems and also because teachers generally do not receive preservice training in these areas. With a school population as significant and as diverse as is the Indian and Metis student population in Saskatchewan, it is obvious that, in order to provide them with a quality education, improvements need to be made in the kinds of training our teachers receive.

2. The distinctive characteristics of spoken Indigenous English are dialectical differences, not evidence of speech deficit or language problem. As well as having implications for teacher preservice and inservice, this also has serious implications for assessment procedures used with second language/dialect children, not to mention the whole issue of standardized instruments being culturally biased. Right now there is a disproportionate number of Indian and Metis students designated as "special needs students". Rather than placing too much emphasis on assessing the remediating, the focus should be shifted to getting on the real business of schools: teaching, reading and writing, regardless of spoken dialect.
3. Differences between cultures go beyond the verbal level. This paper has concentrated on verbal communication and has not even mentioned the other areas that are just as vital to understanding the differences across cultures, i.e. non-verbal communication, communication styles, purposes for which language is used, and differing values, world views and philosophies.
4. Teachers need to examine their own attitudes and assumptions about their students' language. It is important to realize that we convey our attitudes to others at an unconscious level in the same way that we convey to our students our expectations of their performance. This is not intended to blame teachers, rather to inquire whether enough information is being provided by the teacher training programs and institutions regarding varieties of English and appropriate methodologies for second language/dialect teaching.
5. Teachers need to use an additive approach that builds upon and validates the experiences of the Indian and Metis students in their classrooms. This is good teaching for all children. To begin with the child--in this case, with the language of the child--is a basic pedagogical principle. In contrast to the subtractive approach of the past, where attempts were made to eradicate Indigenous

languages and to use English as a tool to assimilate Indian and Metis students, an additive approach does not attempt to change or take away the language that the child brings to school, but seeks to extend and to add to the skills and the language facility that the child already possesses. Ways that teachers can validate the language of their Indian and Metis students include:

a. accepting the language and the culture of the students and fostering that respect among their classmates;
b. modelling and exposing students to standard speech forms but avoiding corrections;
c. establishing an environment where children talk and collaborate with each other;
d. using a learner centered small group approach versus a teacher centered and controlled approach and employing a variety of teaching styles. Rather than relying too heavily on phonics or a structured approach to language and reading, and experiential or whole language approach that utilizes the language and experience of the child is preferred;
e. focusing on language as a meaningful, communicative activity that is used for a purpose, rather than on the form or mechanics of language. In other words, teach students what they can do with language in all its forms rather than focusing on grammar and pronunciation out of context;
f. teaching children that there are many different ways of speaking and that certain forms may be more appropriate in certain situations;
g. adopting aspects of students' speech styles in informal atmospheres to show students that teachers too can switch styles and that they value the students' language enough to incorporate it into the classroom and into their own speech. That step takes with it far greater meaning than just language. it is a cross-cultural teaching skill that carries with it the message "I approve of/respect/like you."

6. Teachers need to become advocates for their Indian and Metis students. In other words, teachers

need to disseminate this information beyond the walls of the classroom to administrators and colleagues. This is necessary in order to dispel the myths of linguistic and cultural deprivation that still exist. It is these myths that are at fault, not the students.

7. The final point is so important that is worth restating - that language, culture, and personality are inseparable. We are all born into speech communities and we all speak like those with whom we wish to identify. Any attempt to negate or change this, no matter who well meaning, will be seen as an attempt to change our personalities and hence devalue the cultures that we come from. The element of choice here is essential. We do want to provide our students with the facility to use standard English when and if they so choose, but not at the expense of their first language or dialect.

For the Indian and Metis student, developing facility with language in as wide a variety as possible of functions, styles, and registers is a means of empowerment, rather than a means of being controlled or assimilated. This is the goal towards which we need to direct language programs for Indian and Metis students, and for all students.

References

Blair, H. and Heit, M. (1987).
Language Needs and Characteristics of Saskatchewan Indian and Metis Students: Implications for Educators. Paper Delivered at the Native American Languages Institute (NALI) Conference. Saskatoon, Saskatchewan.

Blair, H. (1985).
The Relationship of Demographic Characteristics to Teacher Attitudes towards the Oral English of Native Canadian and Aboriginal Australian Children (M.Ed. thesis). Saskatoon, University of Saskatchewan.

Burnaby, B. (1976).
Language in Native Education. Canadian Society for the Study of Education 3: 23-35.

Burnaby, B. (1980). Languages and Their Roles in Educating Native Children. Toronto: OISE Press.

Burnaby, B. (1982).
Language in Education among Canadian Native Peoples. Toronto: OISE Press.

Cohen, A. and Swain, M. (1976). Bilingual Education: The "Immersion" Model in the North American Context. TESOL Quarterly 10: 45-53.

Cummins, J. (1978).
Educational Implications of Mother Tongue Maintenance in Minority Language Groups. Canadian Modern Language Review 34: 395-416.

Cummins, J. (1981).
Bilingualism and Minority Language Children. Toronto: OISE Press.

Cummins, J. (1984).
Bilingualism and Special Education Issues in Assessment and Pedagogy. Clevedon: Multilingual Matters.

Darnell, R. (1979).
Reflections of Cree Interactional Etiquette: Educational Implications. Austin: Southwest Educational Development Laboratory.

Davis, S. (1986).
English/Language Arts Needs Assessment of Indian and Metis Students in Saskatchewan. Unpublished Manuscript. Community Education Branch, Saskatchewan Education.

Fiordo, R. (1985).
The Soft-Spoken Way Versus the Outspoken Way. Journal of American Indian Education 24: 35-48.

Fletcher, J. D. (1983).
What Problems Do American Indians Have with English? Washington, D.C.: Department of Education (ERIC Document ED 247 051)

Freeman, E. B. (1982).
The Ann Arbor Decision: The Importance of Teachers' Attitudes toward Language. The Elementary School Journal 83: 2-21.

Gambell, T. (1987).
A proposed Policy for English/Language Arts K-12 for Saskatchewan Schools. Unpublished Manuscript. Saskatchewan Education, Curriculum Development Division.

Good, T. L. and Brophy, J. E. (1977).
Educational Psychology: A Realistic Approach. New York: Holt, Rinehart and Winston.

Goodman, K. (1986).
What's Whole in Whole Language? Richmond Hill, Ontario: Scholastic-TAB Publications.

Lankford, R. and Riley, J. D. (1986).
Native American Reading Disability. Journal of American Indian Education 25: 1-11.

Reich, B. B. (1978).
The Influence of Cree Language Background on the Perception of English Consonant Phonemes in First Grade Children (M.Ed. thesis). Edmonton, University of Alberta.

Riches, C. J. (1984).
Native English Speaker Reactions to ESL Learner Errors (M.Sc. thesis). Edmonton, University of Alberta.

Shapson, S. and D'Oyley, V. (eds.). (1984).
Bilingual and Multicultural Education: Canadian Perspectives. Clevedon: Multilingual Matters Ltd.

Shrofel, S. (1986).
Differences in Discourse Structure between Native Canadian Indian English and Standard English. Paper Delivered at the Saskatchewan Council for Educators of Non-English Speakers (SCENES) Conference '86.

Shrofel, S. (1987).
Research in First and Second Language Acquisition: What Does It Say and How Can We Match Our Teaching to It? Paper Delivered at the Canadian Association of Second Language Teachers Conference: Regina, Saskatchewan.

Smith, F. (1987).
Keynote Address at the Canadian Association of Second Language Teachers Conference. Regina, Saskatchewan.

Smitherman, G. (ed.). (1981).
Black English and the Education of Black Children and Youth. Detroit: Harlo Press.

Stubbs, M. (1983).
Language, Schools and Classrooms. London: Methuen.

Svenson, K. (1978).
Indian and Metis Issues in Saskatchewan to 2001. Unpublished Manuscript.

Swain, M. (1981).
Bilingual Education for Majority and Minority Language Children. Studia Linguistica 35: 15-32.

Tamaoka, K. (1986).
An Assessment of Congruence between Learning Styles of Cree, Dene, Metis, and Non-Native Students and Instructional Styles of Native and Non-Native Teachers in Selected Northern Saskatchewan Schools (M.Ed. thesis). Saskatoon, University of Saskatchewan.

Toohey, K. (1982).
Northern Native Canadian Second Language Education: A Case Study of Fort Albany, Ontario (Ph.D. thesis). Department of Education, University of Toronto.

Toohey, K. (1985).
Northern Native Canadian Language Education. Canadian Review of Sociology and Anthropology 22: 18-29.

Toohey, K. (1986).
Minority Educational Failure: Is Dialect a Factor? Curriculum Inquiry 16: 34-45.

Trudgill, P. (1975).
Accent, Dialect and the School. London: Edward Arnold Publishers.

Whyte, K. (1986).
Strategies for Teaching Indian and Metis Students. Canadian Journal of Native Education 13:12-25.

TEACHING INSTRUCTIONAL COMMUNICATION TO INDIGENOUS PEOPLE IN ALBERTA

Richard Fiordo and Claudio Violato
University of Calgary

Introduction
Indigenous peoples of North America are frequently misperceived as reticent and taciturn in their oral communication. We hold that under certain conditions, Indigenous people are neither of these but on the contrary, can be affable and articulate. Thus, the benefits of one-way versus two-way models of oral instructional communication in Indigenous (or Indian) education are examined in this paper.

Historically, instructional communication has been conceptualized as one-way (monologue) and two-way (dialogue). Endorsement of two-way models can be found in Plato's Dialogues. Modern support for two-way models appeared in Howe (1963). Matson and Montague (1967: viii) saw dialogue (or two-way communication) as the "path to communion" and monologue (or one-way communication) as the "transmission and reception of stimuli". Seiler, Schuelke, and Lieb-Brilhart (1984) contrasted the lecture method with the discussion method. While the lecture (or one-way model) is an educational speech delivered by one person to a group, discussion (or the two-way model) involves interaction between and among group members. Even though these approaches and methods can be mixed, sometimes better results are obtained from the exclusive use of one method or the other.

The central question of the present study was: Would the two-way model result in longer periods of talk but perceptions that the periods were shorter than the one-way model? McKeachie and Kulik (1975) found that lectures are superior to discussions for learning facts, while discussions are superior to lectures for comprehending, applying synthesizing, and evaluating information. Gage and Berliner (1979) suggested that lectures are as effective as discussions for a number of purposes, such as the dissemination of information and the stimulation of interest in a subject. Lectures, however, are inappropriate when objectives beyond information are desired or when information is very complex, abstract, or detailed. Seiler et al (1984) pointed out that unless teachers volunteer for a continuing self-improvement program in lecturing, their lecturing may become ineffective. For effective lecturing, considerable skills in voice, style, manner, pace, fluency, ease, and orderliness are necessary. Even though discussion requires speaking skills, the degree of skill would be less than (as well as other than) the speaking skills required for the specialized activity of lecturing.

In contrast to the above reports, Stanford and Stanford (1969) found that discussion can help students solve problems, express opinions, discover what others think, express feelings, clarify view points, examine their own opinions, and feel accepted. McKeachie (1978) suggested the use of discussion when educational objectives include using the group members as resources, having students apply principles, gauging objectives by prompt feedback, encouraging students to think about some subject, appraising the logic and evidence of positions set forth, becoming aware of and formulating problems, influencing students in directions counter to previous beliefs, and motivating students to learn. However, McKeachie also warned of several limitations of discussion. Discussants must have adequate information. Discussion can lose its organization and forget its purpose. Instructors may dominate discussions and even answer for the discussants, or may impose agreement on the discussion and its members by insisting that the group must agree. Furthermore, instructors may impose a solution on the group and forcefully implement it.

While the foregoing is a brief review of one-way and two-way communication models, there is a paucity of studies in the fields of instructional communication, intercultural communication and related areas comparing one-way and two-way models of communication with teaching speech communication to Indigenous people. Studies are available on topics pertaining to one-way and two-way communication models in general (Matson and Montague 1967, Fiordo 1985, McKeachie and Kulik 1975, Howe 1963, Beatty, 1986, Knapp and Miller 1985). Studies of spoken proficiency in English can be easily found (Powell 1990, Wong 1985). Research on gender differences in communication style have been done (Staley and Cohen 1988). Intercultural studies of communication are also numerous (Gudykunst and Kim 1984, Burger 1968, Fiordo 1985b, Mallea and Young 1984, Carnew 1984). There appears to be no published study, however, linking one-way and two-way models of speech communication to Indigenous people.

There is also a paucity of studies pertaining to Indigenous people on the subject of communication training. Burger (1968), Carnew (1984), and Bruner (1973) addressed intercultural communication broadly and indirectly in terms of Indigenous education; Greenbaum (1985) examined nonverbal differences in Communication style between American Indian and Anglo elementary classrooms; Mohawk (1985), Toohey (1985), and Harris (1985) studied English language learning and performance among Indigenous people; but none offered specific advice on speech communication training for Indigenous people. Similarly, Gudykunst and Kim (1984), Argyle (1982), and Prosser (1978) addressed intercultural communication specifically and directly, but they did not offer specific advice on speech communication training for Indigenous people. The present study, therefore, was an attempt to explore this specific area of Indigenous education and communication.

Although research on communication apprehension (Ayres 1990, Ayres and Hopf 1990, Beatty and Friedland 1990, McCroskey 1977, Phillips 1977) and self-disclosure (Bourard 1971, Cozby 1972) is plentiful, few studies have consistently measured university Indigenous students on these two factors. Our informal observations of Indigenous students on these factors led us to believe that they had high communication apprehension and generally low self-disclosure, especially when contrasted with their non-Indigenous Canadian counterparts. University Indigenous students appeared to display stagefright to a greater degree than their non-Indigenous counterparts by showing elevated speech anxiety and frequent silence. Employing the one-way model, we had observed that a number of problems arose for Indigenous students. Timing of their speeches was a problem as the students typically fell short of the time requested for their speeches. Subjective reports suggested that the amount of time required to speak was excessive. Students complained whether the time required to speak was 5, 8, or 12 minutes. After presenting their speeches short of the required time or not, the responses were predominantly negative. Such comments as "that 8 minutes seemed like eternity prevailed, even when the actual time speaking was 5 minutes or less".

In the two-way communications model, the time allotted again drew complaints that it was too long. Such remarks as "I never talked for 20 minutes before a class in my life" and "I'll never last 20 minutes in front of a group" were common. Informal observation, however, suggested to us that with two-way communications, the students spoke for longer periods of time but perceived the time to be shorter than was the case. These foregoing general considerations led us to propose and test the following hypothesis: Under two-way models of communications, students would speak for longer periods of time and would perceive the time to be less than was the case, whereas under one-way models, the students would speak for shorter periods of time but would perceive that they spoke for longer periods of time than was the case.

Method

Subjects

A total of 114 subjects participated in the present study and gave presentations which took place in four Indigenous centres in Alberta: Maskwachees Cultural College, AVC-Grouard, Old Sun College, and Ft. Chipewyan. The presentations were required assignments as part of a speech communication course in which all subjects were enroled. The course was a required component of the teacher education program offered by the University of Calgary at these Indigenous centres. A total of 96 presentations using the one-way model were contrasted with 66 presentations using the two-way model. The 96 one-way presentations were delivered by 78 students, 16 males (21%) and 62 females (79%), with a mean age of 28.5. The 66 two-way presentations were delivered by 51 students, 11 males (17%) and 55 females (83%), with a mean age of 27.8.

One-Way Model: Dependent Measures

Communication was operationalized as the total time spent talking (with pauses) before a group from the moment declared as the beginning to the moment declared as the end by the speaker. These assigned presentations varied in length from 5 to 12 minutes: 16 subjects were assigned 12 minutes speeches, 18 subjects 10 minute speeches, 53 subjects 8 minute speeches, 5 subjects 6 minutes speeches, and 4 subjects 5 minute speeches. At the conclusion of each speech, the student recorded the perceived amount of time spoken. Therefore, two dependent measures were obtained: (1) actual time communicating, and (2) perceived time communicating.

Two-Way Model: Dependent Measures

The two-way model aimed at producing an educational outcome that was mutually developed by the teacher and students sharing information cumulatively and progressively through the lesson. The two-way model utilized the spiral notion of interpersonal communication (Dance and Larson 1976): that is, an upward, onward, and outward co-educational communicational lesson.

The students were instructed to present to the class in a conversational manner. They were to proceed by questions, commands, and requests interactively and transactionally. Rather than present information they were asked to elicit it. Instead of having declarative sentences dominate the lesson, the students were told to have interrogative and imperative sentences dominate. Of course, declarative sentences were permitted, but their use was discouraged by instructions. While a lesson plan in an outline form was required, the outline posed questions rather than stated information. One objective of the dialogue approach was to converse with the audience. The conversation was designed to teach through questions. The questions were open, closed, and leading for the most part (Fiordo 1989).

The questions were supposed to yield maximum feedback on the material being taught. As in the one-way model, two dependent measures were obtained: (1) actual time communicating, and (2) perceived time communicating.

Results

With the one-way model, subjects were scored as accurately perceiving their speaking time then they judged correctly within 15 seconds of the actual time. Since the shortest assigned speaking time was 5 minutes, a 30 second error interval (plus/minus 15 seconds) constitutes 10% of the assigned time. This was thought to be a reasonable criterion for accuracy. The same criterion was used in determining the accuracy of the actual speaking time to the assigned time. In the one-way model, the mean time of the perceived error was 62 seconds for above and 28 seconds for below the assigned time. The mean time of the actual error in timing was 28 seconds for above and 46 seconds for below in the assigned time. The numbers and proportions of students speaking above, accurately or below the assigned times and their perceptions are summarized in Table 1.

ONE-WAY	Accuracy	Actual Time***		Perceived Time***	
		Frequency (N)	Percent	Frequency (N)	Percent
	Above	32	33	56	58
	Accurate	9	9	8	9
	Below	55	58	32	33
	Total	96	100	96	100
TWO-WAY**	Accuracy	Actual Time		Perceived Time	
		Frequency (N)	Percent	Frequency (N)	Percent
	Above	48	73	20	30
	Accurate	5	8	12	18
	Below	13	19	34	52
	Total	**66**	**100**	**66**	**100**

Table 1 *Actual and Perceived Time Communicating Within a One-Way or Two-Way Model*

*$X^2 (2)$ = 12.68, p < .01 (actual vs. perceived on one-way)
**$X^2 (2)$ = 23.78, p < .01 (actual vs. perceived on two-way)
***$X^2 (2)$ = 35.06, p < .01 (one-way vs. two-way on perceived)
****$X^2 (2)$ = 18.80, p < .01 (one-way vs. two-way on perceived)

The data from the two-way model are also summarized in Table 1. The dialogue assignment was supposed to take 20 minutes. Accuracy allowed for a 2 minute interval around the assigned 20 minutes. This criterion was selected because as in the one-way model, this interval constitutes 10% of the assigned time. The mean was 2 minutes and 30 seconds for the perceived time above the assigned time. The perceived time below the assigned time had a mean of 3 minutes and 12 seconds. By way of contrast, the actual mean time above the assigned time was 5 minutes and 15 seconds. The actual mean time below the assigned time was 1 minute and 51 seconds.

There was a systematic discrepancy in the actual time speaking and the perceived time with both the one-way model [$X^2(2) = 12.68, p < .01$]

and the two-way model [$X^2(2) = 23.78, p < .01$]. In the one-way model, the students spoke below the actual time a disproportionate number of times (58%) but perceived themselves to have spoken above the assigned time a disproportionate number of times (see Table 1).

In the two-way model, the exact reverse was the case. The students overestimated the above time in 30% of the cases but actually spoke above the time 73% of the cases. Comparing across models further elucidates the patterns of actual versus perceived times. In the one-way model, a disproportionate number of subjects (58%) spoke below the actual time, while in the two-way model only 19% did so. These proportions are statistically significant ($X^2(2) - 35.06, p < .01$). For perceived time, the pattern is reversed. In the one-way model 58% of the subjects thought they spoke above the required time, while in the two-way model only 30% also thought so. Again, this discrepancy is significant ($X^2(2) = 18.80, p < .01$). See Table 1 for a summary. These data quite clearly support the hypothesis that under two-way models of communications, students would speak for longer periods of time and would perceive the times to be less than was the case, whereas under one-way models the students would speak for shorter periods of time but would perceive that they spoke for longer periods of time than was the case.

Discussion and Conclusion

The present study clearly showed that the dialogue method was successful in promoting longer communication among the present subjects. Moreover, they actually tended to underestimate the time they had spoken. The success of this two-way method in getting Indigenous people to talk longer may be due to a number of reasons. It may have to do with the advantage the students have in managing conversations (Cappella 1985), the social power available to the students through the dialogue form of interpersonal communication (Berger 1985), the influence the students can extend interpersonally through the two-way model (Siebold, Cantrill, and Meyers 1985), or even the interpersonal competence that is potential in conversational approach (Parks 1985). Any of these may be the primary factor underlying the positive results. It might also be cultural factors unique to Indigenous communities (Burger 1968, Carnew 1984, Bruner 1973), related to Indigenous values pertaining to cooperation (Pelletier 1970), the general use of Indigenous languages (Parker 1975, Tough 1976) dealing with shared ethnic backgrounds and customs (Government of the Northwest Territories 1981, Mallea and Young 1984), modelling and role-playing (McDougall 1985), and unique traditional Indigenous ways of learning and relating

(Couture 1985). Finally, one may speculate that the students were too busy to be self-conscious and suffer stagefright. By being lost in their dialogical lesson, they were free of the contaminating effects of being preoccupied with delivery. Our informal observations suggest to us that the same comparative effects of one-way versus two-way models occur with non-Indigenous speakers. Thus, the last interpretation seems to be favoured at this time. In any case, further research should be conducted to test these various possibilities.

The results of the present study are subject to an important caveat. The criterion for accuracy on timing was guided by contextual considerations. Since we had no guidance from previous research on timing accuracy, on the basis of previous observations, we decided on a range of 15 seconds for the one-way assignments since these were assignments at a minimum of 5 minutes. Following similar reasoning we also decided on a arrange of 2 minutes on the two-way assignments because these were 20 minute assignments. Given the array of unpredictable distractions that occurred under these speech communication circumstances, the 15 second leeway for the monologues and 2 minute leeway for the dialogues served us in a practicable manner since both of these constituted 10% of the assigned time.

Although the reasons for the increase in speech production are not completely clear at this point, it is likely that the dialogical method will yield positive results with Indigenous people. While further research along this line is encouraged - especially systematic empirical research - the two-way model for teaching speech communication to Indigenous people seems workable and sound. Further research into this approach would benefit the teaching and research communities by adding empirical precision to the exploration of this study. Meanwhile the two-way model of speech communication described in this study serves as one method to assist teachers of Indigenous students to elicit lengthy presentations from their students.

References

Argyle, M. (1982).
Intercultural Communication. In S. Bochner (ed.), *Cultures in Contact*, 23-35. New York: Pergamon.

Ayres, J. (1990).
Goal Incongruence: A Source of Public Speaking Anxiety. *Journal of the Northwest Communication Association* 18: 26-40.

Ayres, J., and Hopf, T .S. (1990).
The Long-Term Effect of Visualization in the Classroom: A Brief Research Report. *Communication Education* 39: 75-78.

Beatty, M. J. (1986).
Romantic Dialogue: Communication in Dating and Marriage. Englewood: Morton.

Beatty, M. J., and Friedland, M. H. (1990).
Public Speaking State Anxiety as a Function of Selected Situational and Predispositional Variables. *Communication Education* 39: 142-147.

Berger, C. R. (1985).
Social Power and Interpersonal Communication. In M. L. Knapp and G. R. Miller (eds.), *Handbook of Interpersonal Communication*, 439-499. London: Sage.

Bruner, J. (1973).
Culture, Politics, and Pedagogy. In F. Ianni and E. Storey (eds.), *Cultural Relevance and Educational Issues*, 45-58. Boston: Little, Brown, and Company.

Burger, H. S. (1968).
Ethnopedagogy: A Manual in Cultural Sensitivity with Techniques for Improving Cross-Cultural Teaching by Fitting Ethnic Patterns. Albuquerque: Southwestern Cooperative Education Laboratory.

Cappella, J. N. (1985).
The Management of Conversations. In M. L. Knapp and G. R. Miller (eds.), *Handbook of Interpersonal Communication*, 393-438. London: Sage.

Carnew, F. (1984).
Toward Policy in Indigenous Education. *Multicultural Education Journal* 2: 4-18.

Couture, J. E. (1985).
Traditional Indigenous Thinking, Feeling, and Learning. *Multicultural Education Journal* 3: 4-16.

Cozby, P. (1972).
Self-Disclosure, Reciprocity, and Liking. *Sociometry* 35: 151-160.

Dance, F. E., and Larson, C. E. (1976).
The Functions of Human Communication. New York: Holt, Rinehart and Winston.

Fiordo, R. (1985a).
The Participation Project at the University of Calgary: Innovative Approaches to Increasing Student Participation in the Basic Speech Communication Course. *Education Canada* 12: 30-34.

Fiordo, R. (1985b).
The Soft-Spoken vs. the Outspoken Way: A Bicultural Approach to Teaching Speech Communication. *Journal of American Indian Education* 24: 35-48.

Fiordo, R. (1989).
The Semiotic Sea of Questioning. *Semiotica* 73: 25-41.

Gage, N. L. and Berliner, D. (1979).
Educational Psychology. Boston: Houghton Mifflin.

Government of Northwest Territories, Department of Education. (1981).
Bilingual Education: An Overview and Recommendations Yellowknife: Programs and Evaluation Branch.

Greenbaum, P. E. (1985).
Nonverbal Differences in Communication Style between American Indian and Anglo Elementary Classrooms. *American Education Research Journal* 22: 101-115.

Gudykunst, W. B., and Kim, Y. Y. (1984).
Communicating with Strangers: An Approach to Intercultural Communication. New York: Random House.

Harris, G. A. (1985).
Considerations in Assessing English Language Performance of Indigenous American Children. *Topics in Language Disorders* 5: 45-52.

Howe, R. L. (1963).
The Miracle of Dialogue. New York: The Seabury Press.

Jourard, S. M. (1971).
Self-disclosure: An experimental analysis of transparent self. New York: John Wiley.

Knapp, M. L., and Miller, G. R. (1985).
Handbook of Interpersonal Communication. London: Sage.

Mallea, J. R., and Young, J. C. (1984).
Cultural Diversity and Canadian Education: Issues and Innovations. Ottawa: Carleton University.

Martin, J. (1983).
Mastering Instruction. Toronto: Allyn and Bacon.

Matson, F.W., and Montague, A. (eds.). (1967).
The Human Dialogue: Perspectives on Communication. New York: The Free Press.

McCroskey, J. C. (1977).
Classroom Consequences of Communication Apprehension. *Communication Education* 26: 27-33.

McDougall, D. (1985).
Teaching Empathy and the Reduction of Prejudice. *Multicultural Education Journal* 3: 5-13.

McKeachie, W. J. (1978).
Teaching Tips: A Guidebook for the Beginning College Teacher. Lexington, Mass.: D.C. Heath.

McKeachie, W. J., and Kulik, J. A. (1975).
Effective College Teaching. In F. N. Kerlinger (ed.), *Review of Research in Education,* Vol.3 3446-478. Washington, D.C.: American Education Research Association.

Mohawk, J. C. (1985).
Seeking a Language of Understanding. Social Education 49: 104-105.

Parker, D. V. (1975).
Language, Policy, and Indian Education. Edmonton: Northern Development Group.

Parker, M. R. (1985).
Interpersonal Communication and the Quest for Personal Competence. In M. L. Knapp and G. R. Miller (eds.), *Handbook of Interpersonal Communication,* 171-204. London: Sage.

Pearson, J. Nelson, P. E. (1982).
Understanding and Sharing: An Introduction to Speech Communication. Dubuque: W. C. Brown.

Pearson, J. C. (1985).
Gender and Communication. Dubuque: W. C. Brown.

Pelletier, W. (1970).
Childhood in an Indian Village. In S. Repo (ed.), *This Book Is about Schools,* 23-32. New York: Vintage Books.

Phillips, G. M. (1977).
Rhetoritherapy Versus the Medical Model: Dealing with Reticence. *Communication Education* 26: 34-43.

Powell, R. G. (1990).
Measuring Minimal Proficiency in Spoken English. *Communication Reports* 3: 37-44.

Prosser, M. (1978).
The Cultural Dialogue. Boston: Houghton Mifflin.

Seiler, W. J., Schuelke, L. D., and Lieb-Brilhart, B. (1984).
Communication for the Contemporary Classroom. New York: Holt, Rinehart and Winston.

Siebold, D. R., Cantrill, J. G., and Meyers, R. A. (1985).
Communication and Interpersonal Influence. In M. L. Knapp, G .R. Miller (eds.), *Handbook of Interpersonal Communication,* 551-614. London: Sage.

Staley, C. C., and Cohen, J. L. (1988).
Communication Strategies and Social Style: Similarities and Differences between the Sexes. *Communication Quarterly* 36: 192-202.

Stanford, G. and Stanford, B. D. (1969).
Learning Discussion Skills through Games. New York: Citation Press.

Toohey, K. (1985).
English as a Second Language for Indigenous Canadians. *Canadian Journal of Education* 10: 273-293.

Tough, J. (1976).
Listening to Children Talking. London: Ward Lock Educational.

Wong, R. (1985).
Does Pronunciation Teaching Have a Place in the Communication Classroom? In D. E. Tannen and J. Alatis (eds.), *Languages and Linguistics: The Interdependence of Theory, Data, and Application,* 34-45. Washington, D.C.: Georgetown University Press.